Executive Information Systems
From Proposal Through Implementation

Wayne C. Burkan

VNR VAN NOSTRAND REINHOLD
New York

Copyright © 1991 by Van Nostrand Reinhold

Library of Congress Catalog Card Number 90-20480
ISBN 0-442-00437-0

Manufactured in the United States of America

Published by Van Nostrand Reinhold
115 Fifth Avenue
New York, New York 10003

Chapman and Hall
2-6 Boundary Row
London, SE 1 8HN

Thomas Nelson Australia
102 Dodds Street
South Melbourne 3205
Victoria, Australia

Nelson Canada
1120 Birchmount Road
Scarborough, Ontario M1K 5G4, Canada

16 15 14 13 12 11 10 9 8 7 6 5 4 3 2 1

Library of Congress Cataloging-in-Publication Data

Burkan, Wayne C.
    Executive information systems : from proposal through implementation /
Wayne C. Burkan.
        p.   cm.
    Includes index.
    ISBN 0-442-00437-0
    1. Management information systems.   I. Title.
    T58.6.B874   1991
658.4'038--dc20   90-20480
                                             CIP

To Martha
She has stood by me through years of insane travel. Now she has supported me through the rigors of preparing this book. I could not be more fortunate.

Contents

Preface

Four years ago I stated that most executive information sytems were failing. They had failed not only in spite of people's best efforts, but often *because of their efforts*. This outcome was avoidable then, and it is even more avoidable today. EIS can make an enormous contribution to an organization's future. The techniques described in this book are dedicated to that future.

"Failures" of technology have been quite common throughout history— every major innovation starts out with a lot of hype and hope. Within a few years, the euphoria is replaced with disappointment and cynicism. If the technology proves itself, however, the cynicism eventually yields to reality and success. The automobile, the radio, television, and personal computers have all experienced such an acceptance cycle. Now executive information systems are having their turn at bat.

There is little doubt that this innovation holds tremendous potential for many organizations. Business periodicals around the world have published numerous stories on the benefits and successes of EIS. The number of EIS vendors has doubled in less than two years, and this growth seems explosive. Yet already we are beginning to see articles in the popular press concerning the unfulfilled promise of EIS.

This book is dedicated to exploring the practical aspects of what causes the success and failure of executive information systems, and how to translate that knowledge into action. It gives particular emphasis to four major areas: understanding your needs (and their implications), conducting the executive interview, understanding the differences in EIS technologies, and conducting the evaluation.

The treatment of all topics has been designed for the busy practitioner, to ensure quick and useful reading. Try to resist the temptation to jump directly to a chapter that interests you today. The material builds on itself. Even if you have already completed some of the earlier stages of an EIS project, I urge you to tackle the material in order.

Executive information systems can have an extraordinary impact on organizations. An EIS can dramatically improve an executive's ability to move an organization in new directions, can enhance the management and control of key resources, and can reward both private and public sector leadership with significant productivity gains. This book is dedicated to the realization of these visions.

One final comment: throughout this book I have deliberately used nonstandard terminology, rather than borrow terms from information systems. My experience is that even where the technical meaning of terms is identical, the IS application is heavily skewed toward traditional systems development and mainframe processing. Were I to define the IS terms and explain their nuances, I would run the risk of reinforcing the very paradigms I am attempting to break.

part I
for the
executive

1

The Value of Information

During an interview with the CEO of a large manufacturing company, I asked what his most valuable source of information was. Without delay he responded that meetings were by far the most valuable. That was not unusual. In fact, after hundreds of such interviews, I would say it was the most common response. The vigor of his answer impressed me, however, so I questioned him as to why. "Because," he responded, "at meetings all the information is tailored to me." In that one sentence he captured the essence of the problem with information today.

Most of the information an executive receives is mass-produced, historical (reflects past events) and inwardly focused, thus giving the executive a limited perspective. The limits are not due to an inherent problem with MIS, but rather reflect the necessary requirements of developing fundamental and low-level accounting systems. Once these systems are operational, however, the incremental value of the information they generate, from a management point of view, decreases over time.

The general ledger, for example, represents extremely important information to every senior-level manager. Every improvement to the ledger, however, begins to represent a diminishing return of information value. Whenever a new information system is developed, there is a natural tendency to view information needs in that mold. The organization naturally migrates *within* the established information paradigm, rarely jumping to new paradigms.

Information has four primary functions:

- Mandated
- Control
- Management
- Leadership

Compulsion causes the first; tactical survival dictates the second. The first two functional requirements so dominate our information that most organizations are unaware of the value of information relating to the second two. Efforts to *refine* our fundamental systems typically result in an incremental improvement. Although this improvement may increase control, it rarely enhances the executive's ability to make any significant impact on the organization. Perhaps this is why many executives seem to feel they are "spending more but enjoying it less."

Most of the improvements in information delivery have concentrated on internal information, but our increasing burden of challenges comes from outside forces. The best-run IS departments seem to have provided marginal disutility in attempting to move information toward management or leadership. That is, the more we become overburdened with the sheer volume of reports, the greater our risk of missing the truly important information.

Most executives with whom I have worked have responded to this overload problem by selecting a small, core set of reports from which to draw. For one faced with the alternative of sifting through mountains of reports, this is a simple, survival solution. The more the reports increase in volume (and they always do), the more executives draw on this circle-the-wagons approach. They recognize that they run the risk of missing some valuable information, but reason that "I can't read everything." They become increasingly reliant on meetings and informal verbal exchanges to fill in the missing pieces of the business.

Formal and informal verbal exchanges are an important source of information for all executives. Formal and informal meetings, phone calls, office visits, and "walking around," however, all suffer from the same inherent limitations:

- Retrieval at some later date becomes memory-dependent.
- Identifying patterns is very difficult.

- We become reliant on information tailored to us. The good news is that it is more easily consumed; however, "looking under the covers" then becomes that much more difficult.

- Information that people want you to have is much more easily obtained than information with which they prefer that you not get too familiar.

- People rarely walk around talking about strategic issues; so this is precisely the type of information that gets the lowest exposure.

Executive information systems are not a replacement for verbal sources of information, nor are they intended totally to replace traditional reporting. They represent a third alternative, one that offers a strong complement to traditional information exchange. Although they can (and do) enhance the value of mandated and control-type information, perhaps their greatest value is in advancing the management and control of the organization.

MANAGEMENT

The management use of information reflects our ability to minimize surprise. Its effectiveness is measured in our ability to *see and anticipate,* both short term and long term. It is precisely because control systems are inwardly focused that their enhancement actually diminishes an executive's ability to manage. Our ability to anticipate is measured in our vision of the organization's environment, and its perspective of time as it relates to the future.

Peter Drucker pointed out that anticipation has little value if you "are standing on top of a mountain with twenty mile visibility." If the clouds roll in, and the weather becomes "turbulent," he continued, management either anticipates, or dies. Many organizations understand that they have entered turbulent times. The need for new management information has never been greater.

LEADERSHIP

If management is our ability to see the future, leadership is our ability to *shape* the future. It is measured by how well we can move the organization's resources to new directions. The most important of these resources, of course, is employees. The better our ability to quickly redirect our employees, the better we can shape our future.

Information has a very natural and profound influence on employees. They will gravitate toward positive recognition and away from negative recognition. Because information systems are capable of creating this recognition, it follows that information can have a direct influence on employee behavior. Conversely, a lack of information leaves this recognition to formal and informal standards. These standards may be historically justified, but at best they are unrelated to moving the organization in new directions.

EIS AND INFORMATION VALUE

Executive information systems are far more than just the electronic delivery of reports and graphs. If the technology appears trivial, it is because it has all-too-often been implemented as trivial. The emphasis needs to be shifted away from the computer and toward the business issues every executive is struggling to address.

An EIS offers us a very real opportunity to contribute to executive effectiveness on virtually every level. It can monitor our progress toward such critical goals as quality, customer service, innovation, employee empowerment, and reduced cycle-time. Moving beyond merely monitoring conditions, however, the EIS can significantly leverage our efforts to move our organizations closer to these goals.

2

The Technology Paradox

They had bought into the new technology amid considerable fanfare and hype. They expected productivity gains. More, they expected to celebrate new applications never possible with the old technology. The economic justification for their decision seemed overwhelming.

Instead, their high hopes had turned to cynicism. Increasingly, they began to suspect that once again, technology had let them down. We are not describing computers, nor are we referring to factory automation. The technology in this case was the truck, in the year 1907. So great was the disappointment with this promising new technology, that the following advertisement for the International Commercial Truck appeared:

That the motor truck is an excellent substitute for the horse has been proven in every instance where business men have given it a fair trial. But the man who uses his motor truck simply as a substitute for horses neglects to make the most of his opportunities. The horse is not a machine—five to six hours actual work — fifteen to twenty-five miles—is its maximum day's work. A motor truck can be used twenty-four hours a day if necessary, and it will travel the last hour and the hundredth mile just as fast as the first.

Business men who are using the motor truck in place of horse and wagon equipment with the great success are men who have given this problem careful study. In most instances it was necessary to change the plan of

routing—delays which were necessary to give the horses rest were elimi-
nated—plans were laid to keep the truck busy the entire day with as few
delays as possible. . . .[1]

This was not a unique experience. Virtually every new technology suffers through a period of the paradigm effect.[2] A result of what Joel Barker
calls "hardening of the categories," the paradigm effect is the inability to
see the world through anything other than your old framework.

The early radio was referred to as the "wireless." Seen by most as a
replacement for the telephone, it initially was applied to personal (person-
to-person) communications. It was only much later that the use of broad-
casting (communication to large groups) became popular.

This is precisely the bind we find ourselves in today. After decades of
incredible increases in power, the computer continues to find most of its
applications rooted in processing speed: doing essentially what we have
always done, the way we have always done it—the only difference being
speed.

The introduction of personal computing into the corporate mentality
was accompanied by a newly identified old concept, that of the paperless
office. Once again we created boundaries for the new technology that were
based on old applications. With few exceptions, computers were praised
for their liberating potential, while applied to such limited-potential jobs
as word processing, spreadsheet calculations, and database manipulation.

After more than a decade, little has changed. It can be argued, in fact,
that we have actually taken a few steps back. For example, we no longer
refer to the paperless office. Instead we speak of office automation, rele-
gating this powerful technology to merely automating that which we
historically have done manually.

The news is not all bleak. Some database applications are allowing us
to improve our understanding of the customer, and respond more rapidly
to our customer's needs. Our understanding of production has improved,
and with it our competitiveness.

Unfortunately, much of computing (and specifically office automation)
is still grounded in the old processing paradigm of the 1950s. Recent
developments do little to increase one's optimism. The popularity of desktop publishing, for example, moves us from the "faster is better" paradigm
to the "prettier is better" paradigm. In neither instance do we fundamentally question the basic role of computing as a faster, perhaps more artistic
pen.

One of the first word processors on the market was The Electronic Pencil,
perhaps the first harbinger of things to come. In the ensuing decade, we
improved the technology manyfold. Why is it, then, that many organi-

zations have found themselves cutting back on information systems expenditures? Could it be that we are becoming disenchanted with technology's answer to the truck? Maybe we will soon see this advertisement from one of the leading computer vendors: "Stop using your computer like a pen."

THE CHALLENGE

The challenge of white collar computing is not to replicate our existing capabilities, but to extend those capabilities and leverage them off our enormous human potential. Computing should not be demeaning; it can and should be liberating. To this end, we need to reexamine even our most fundamentally held paradigms concerning business, information, and technology.

Data is like signals from our nervous system. Such signals are of primary importance, for without them existence ceases. During the 1960s the push in computing was the production of data—a quite appropriate goal, given the virtual lack of even the most fundamental signals within the organizational "body."

When we were well into the 1970s, we realized that we had enough data. We were able to sustain the organizational body, but not to advance it. The abundance of signals we had created needed to be organized. What we needed was not just data, but organized data. This need gave birth to the popularity of management reports, or data with perspective.

Do you remember the Greek myth of the Aegean stables? The more they were shoveled, the more they filled. Computing during the seventies and eighties was much like this. Executives would shovel through dozens of reports, only a fraction of which would produce some insight. That insight would highlight areas of concern, which in turn would generate still more reports.

Perhaps even more pernicious is the reporting support structure. For every number on the report, a dozen, a hundred, perhaps even a thousand numbers needed to be calculated. As competitive and operational pressures increased, so also did the number of reports increase (both useful and useless). Each report required more numbers to feed it. As the volume of reports began to reach a critical mass, the demand for IS resources to support the reporting "demand" continued to grow, while the ability of the system to respond quickly continued to diminish.

The executive would receive the required report, but the price for such information was steep. Reporting had become a Faustian contract: short-term gain, long-term pain.

The transition from data to information was measured in our ability to add perspective to data, and here we were successful. Ironically, however, this information flow was bottom–up. It represented neither the needs of executive management, nor those of their support staff. As one frustrated IS director explained, "I don't know *what* he wants, so I give him everything."

THE APPROACH

We mentioned earlier that we can think of management reporting as data with perspective, or information. Unfortunately, the perspective is often that of the organization's lowest level feeder systems, or what Peter Drucker calls the "faint, unfocused signals that pass for communication."

Executive management does not need information, it needs insight. Such insight is information with perspective—the executive's perspective. True, information (management reports) is a necessary building block, as is data; but information suffers from the same basic limitations that afflict data.

People naturally search for patterns, and they gain insight by completing those patterns. With too much information, or unfocused information, pattern recognition becomes increasingly difficult. We find ourselves in the paradoxical situation that the more information we provide to executive management, the lower is the likelihood that we will create insight.

THE SOLUTION

How do we create insight? One popular solution is to limit the information that the executive sees. This is solving the wrong problem. The problem is not that management sees too much information, but that the information executives do see is unfocused for their needs. Limiting this information should not be confused with providing a focused information system to executives.

As we strive for excellence in leadership, we must remember that it is essentially an outgoing, future-oriented activity. Executive management is charged with the responsibility of adding value to this process; yet many of our signals are based on historical, internal, and unfocused information.

Every executive must take responsibility for altering the information flow of his or her organization. We can no longer afford the bottom–up approach to information. We must shift the paradigm born of decades of traditional management philosophy. Gone are the days when we can be satisfied being passive consumers of information. We must become actively involved in shaping information specific to our needs. Today's executives must become the information advocates of the 1990's.

REFERENCES

1. This advertisement was found in Maine's Owls Head Transportation Museum.

2. Joel Arthur Barker, *Discovering the Future: The Business of Paradigms,* I.L.I. Press, Minnesota, 1989.

3

Organizational Issues

Ultimately technology is not just a question of machines and systems, but of power and how power is allocated ...
                    Karen Nussbaum "Office Automation: Jekyll or Hyde?"

Delivering information to the executive has its share of technical challenges, but they pale when compared to the political issues surrounding such an endeavor. We need to identify the issues, stakes, and stakeholders, and to plan specific courses to diminish the chance of conflict.

EXECUTIVE ISSUES

Many executives enthusiastically embrace the concept of EIS. It is not unusual to hear of situations where a director or vice president of MIS is told to "get me one!" by a senior executive. This individual is the most obvious player in the game, perhaps the ultimate stakeholder. So it is surprising to some that, in other cases, the person with the most to gain could rationally resist (and sometimes sabotage) direct delivery of information. What causes this resistance?

Fear of Failure

Some executives are deeply concerned about their ability to master the technology. Rather than appear "foolish," they would prefer to resist the new. This resistance can range from simple avoidance to actively trying to torpedo the project ("I know it will not work, and I won't allow my people to waste their time participating!").

Sometimes this fear dissipates naturally as the executive sees other nontechnical managers mastering the technology with ease. Once the line is drawn, however, such individuals often continue to defend their original position, blocking progress at every turn. At best they may never buy into the project. At worst, they can become an active obstacle to the resources required to make the system work quickly and smoothly.

A popular cure for such technophobia is to demonstrate the technology's ease of use. During one presentation a wary executive jumped up after seeing how touching the screen could replace typing on keys. "That," he exclaimed, thrusting his finger at an imaginary computer screen, "I can do!"

Another approach is fashioned after the old Life cereal commercials, where the product's the true tastiness was determined by asking a finicky Mikey to try it. "Let Mikey try it . . . he doesn't like anything." If you can identify and persuade a technology-hostile executive to try the new technology, you greatly lower the likelihood of fear-based resistance.

Long Memories

Information systems may have a history of projects long on promise and short on delivery. If IS lacks credibility, the EIS project may also suffer the fate of embedded cynicism. Guilt by association can be just as damning as guilt by commission.

The best solution here is to show how the "new" approach is different from what has preceded it. This may not be easy, but it is undoubtedly the best option in trying to win over a recalcitrant executive.

Naturally, you can also try to appeal to the executive's appreciation of the benefits of the technology. Most often, however, concerns over risk outweigh any expectation of benefit. That is why making a joint case for benefits and low risk is your best bet.

Where possible, it is always a good idea not to exclude any executive from the EIS process. Resistant executives should be invited to all presentations, included in interview plans, and kept advised of all progress. Well-intentioned implementation teams sometimes set upon a strategy of exclusion of such unenlightened individuals. This serves only to increase the gap between the players. There are no winners, and the organization is the clear loser.

PROVIDER ISSUES

Most people do not fear technology, but rather the implications of that technology. For those who currently provide information to the executive, this fear can range from loss of prestige to loss of employment. The concerns are real, and must be addressed in a careful and sensitive manner.

Loss of Employment

Peter Drucker asserts that many middle managers are merely "relays for the faint, unfocused signals that pass for communication." Automated reporting puts at risk these "relays," who add little to the information process. If such a person has been designated as an information provider, then the concern over loss of employment can be very real.

There are no documented cases where an EIS has precipitated layoffs, but this may be small comfort to persons who see themselves at risk. Several organizations have reported that they have been able to better manage after downsizing because of these systems.

Anyone thus at risk can be expected to vigorously resist any attempt at automation. Such employees need to understand their place in the post-EIS organization, and to expect that such a move holds at least the promise of an improvement. Without such security, the implementation team can do little but charge ahead in the face of the resistance.

Loss of Influence

We all like to think we have a real ability to impact the decision making process of the organization. Information providers are no different. Part of their "psychic income" is from the opportunity (real or imagined) to have such an impact.

Properly implemented, there is no risk to this group. The EIS, in fact, can actually enhance their ability to influence their direction of the organization. This reality will not replace the fear, however, without careful communication on all parts.

Some people are not seeking influence as much as visibility, the opportunity to be recognized by the senior executive. They see the EIS as robbing them of recognition. At best they will not participate in the process. At worst, they will actively fight its progress.

The EIS gives the information provider, who adds value to what is communicated, the opportunity for more visibility, and an enhanced ability to influence the direction of the organization. Color coding, drill down, and commentary all provide an expanded opportunity to impact the decision making process, sometimes in ways never before possible (see Chapter 13). Many EIS implementations offer enhanced visibility by placing the provider's name directly on the screen of information for which they are responsible. This gives the executive the ability to directly query those responsible for the information, effectively shortening the information lag. At the same time, the provider is given a new level of executive recognition.

ORGANIZATIONAL DEVELOPMENT

In recent months, I have noticed a new force in the organizational tug-of-war. Many companies have organizational development (OD), a group chartered to help the organization move in new directions. Such directions include employee empowerment, enhanced customer service, attention to quality, and renewed innovativeness.

Occasionally some within OD become alarmed over the prospect of a system designed primarily to deliver information to the executive suite. The concept sounds alarmingly elitist. They reason, "Wouldn't the resources be better spent increasing information availability to all employees, rather than concentrating on a select few?" They worry about the use of EIS to control employees. They see the risk of more centralization, less autonomy, and are threatened by the vulnerability inherent in empowerment.

There is no guarantee that the EIS will not be abused in ways that confirm OD's worst fears, and there are undoubtedly cases where this has happened. A strong case can be made, however, for the EIS as supporting the OD process. The EIS can, after all, provide powerful new ways to consistently signal the organization about the new directions it wants to follow. The data feeding the EIS can be used by management and employees alike to measure progress toward their goals. Finally, the EIS can give senior management the ability to monitor the progress of the OD effort itself.

IS ISSUES

There should be little doubt that EIS is a paradigm shift in organizational computing. As with any paradigm shift, many of the old rules become obsolete, and much of the old investment becomes worthless. The history of computing is a history of progress against resistance. End user computing, personal computing, fourth generation languages, LANs and CASE have all experienced more than their share of resistance within the ranks of information systems. This resistance is certainly not universal. Many IS professionals are forward-thinking and accepting of change and its implications. But there has always been a core group that vigorously resists the new paradigm.

EIS turns many of the old rules on their heads. We move from mass production to customization, from centralized planning to decentralized execution, from accuracy to "good enough." Programming skills are replaced by communication skills, and throwaway applications become high priority. Just as the big-three television networks have discovered that the old rules are increasingly worthless in the new paradigm of cable and video productions, the traditionalists in IS are finding the old order once again under attack.

There is little doubt that hostile members of the IS profession can do a great deal of harm to an IS project. They may not "own" the data, but they certainly do control much of the most prized information. Further, they supply critical support skills such as connectivity, communications, hardware support, and data access. Withholding any of these skills can seriously injure the EIS process.

There is another form of IS sabotage which is often well intentioned, but always dangerous. Just as lawmakers put "riders" on priority bills up for a vote, members of the IS community may see the EIS proposal as a way to get funding for a pet project. The funding request jumps almost overnight to include a new mainframe or "support software." The head-count request may triple "to allow for the overhaul of the general ledger."

We are not questioning the merits of any of these add-on projects. They may be quite valuable on their own. Unless the EIS *directly and unavoidably* depends on an add-on as a precondition, however, its inclusion can delay and even derail the executive system.

How can you avoid potential problems within MIS? The best option is straight education—not just education on what you are planning to do, but *why* you chose the approach you selected.

A second step is to include MIS in all important decisions, and be sure it has representation on the EIS team. This is not done just for the obvious political benefits. It also recognizes the very significant contribution MIS can and must make if the EIS project is to enjoy sustainable, long-term success.

CONCLUDING THOUGHTS

Any team effort involving diverse backgrounds and interests is bound to provoke a challenging discussion. The work of the EIS team is no exception. To keep the discussion from degrading into a brawl, it is quite helpful to come to a common understanding of how the project will measure success and failure. The executive may define success as quick response to his or her needs. The provider may measure success by the amount of analysis available to the executive. Both analysis and speed are vital, but they may ultimately conflict.

If the team agrees on priorities and tradeoffs, almost any other issue becomes trivial by comparison. If these discussions do not take place, or if agreement cannot be reached, these measures will produce perpetual problems and crises.

4

Common Wisdom, Common Myths

With any new technology, myths abound as pioneer practitioners attempt to discover the new rules. Not surprisingly, many of these "new" rules are simply the old rules applied to the new technology. If that were the end of it, the usefulness of a chapter on common wisdom and myths would be quite limited.

Unfortunately, these same pioneer practitioners are the ones who are quoted by the press, participate in technical conferences as "experts," and host visits by organizations hoping to build on the pioneers' insights. Further contributing to the proliferation of this "common wisdom," the technology vendors rush to absorb these gems of knowledge into their literature, thus demonstrating their grasp of the new rules.

The net result of this communal education is a dizzying proliferation of commonly accepted rules and standards that all too often lead the industry down a very misguided path. By the time the new rules are discovered for what they are, the technology battlefield is littered with the bodies of those who tried and failed. The same press that helped to promote the flawed rules now jumps on the stories of lost productivity, cost overruns, and failed applications.

This is not intended to represent a complete reference for the myths of EIS. I have included some of the more injurious rules, which are a direct result of applying valid paradigms to inappropriate circumstances.

ACCURACY AND THE HOLY GRAIL

There are many ways to die, some more grisly than others; but none is more grisly than to deliver inaccurate information to an executive. Beyond all else, only deliver the highest accuracy through your EIS. So says the common wisdom (CW).

This advice ranks among the most damaging. The logic and its application work as follows:

CW: Only deliver information of the highest accuracy. To do otherwise would frustrate the executive, and destroy the credibility of the system.

Application: Prioritize the information that is the most accurate. Avoid any information whose accuracy cannot be substantiated.

Implications: The EIS quickly fills with the data most matching these characteristics. Historical data is typically quite accurate. It fits nicely into this paradigm. Within this classification, financial, sales, and other operation indicators top the list.

Consequences: The executive users see predominantly or exclusively that information consisting of hard, historical, and operational data. The good news is that this information is quite abundant. The bad news is that it offers little added value to the user over paper reports. Because of supply/push reporting (Figure 4-1), this is the same basic information that has always been delivered.

Surprisingly, many organizations do not see this approach as precluding executive interviews. They will conduct the interview using their standard approach, but filter out any expressed requirements that fail to match the accuracy paradigm. These requested outliers will be put on the shelf, not accurate enough for inclusion.

What kind of information becomes disenfranchised? Often the very information holding the highest potential for added value is left out. We find ourselves in a catch-22: information on competitive intelligence, customer service, quality, employee empowerment, innovation, cycle time, and anticipation have not historically existed, let alone been provided to the executive suite. Because the information has not benefited from twenty years of refinement, it could never measure up to the accuracy yardstick. Some categories of data, in fact, may *never* be deemed accurate. Would

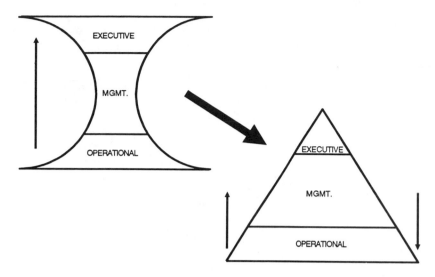

Supply/push reporting summarizes data from operational systems, only to again explode the information flow to the executive level.

Demand/pull dramatically reduces the need for standard reporting by providing the executive with easy access to a wide range of potentially critical . . . without intervention.

Figure 4-1. Push vs. pull reporting.

you ever expect to see accurate competitive intelligence? By its very nature, this data is quite likely to be inaccurate. Few executives, however, would want to be shielded from such potentially valuable insight.

The problem with the accuracy paradigm is that it is inappropriately applied, with the tail wagging the dog. Value does not come from accuracy. For some classes of data, only the strictest standards can be employed; but for others, we need to greatly liberalize our definition of accuracy. Ask any executive how she or he views the accuracy/value tradeoff. The answer may surprise you.

INFORMATION DELIVERED IN THIRTY MINUTES OR LESS

The pitfalls associated with the accuracy paradigm are severely compounded by the CW that fast EIS delivery to the executive is critical.

CW—The EIS is a prototype and will change rapidly. Do not worry about getting the content "perfect"; just deliver something as fast as possible.

Application—Prioritize the content based on availability. The easier the data is to access, the faster you can get your system delivered.

Implications—The most electronically accessible and abundant data in any organization is strikingly similar to data we filtered by applying the accuracy yardstick— historical and operational.

Consequences—We satisfy the executives' lowest level expectations. The technology may wow them, but the content rarely will. At best, they may be impressed by the delivery; at worst, they will utter those dreaded five words, "Is that all there is?"

Like accuracy, this CW is flawed in its application. It is important to deliver your EIS fast, but it is far more important to deliver value. These two need not be in conflict. It is not necessary to deliver *only* high-added-value data. A reasonable standard is to at least deliver an hors d'oeuvre with the main course.

Much of the highest value information will be difficult to access. Because its inclusion would significantly slow delivery, it will be postponed. Thoughtful examination of the alternatives, however, usually identifies several high value data types that can be delivered in short order.

For a southern manufacturing organization, the status of major engineering projects was considered vital. Although the data existed electronically (in microcomputer spreadsheets), it was never part of the formal reporting process. Inclusion in the EIS was not a technical challenge, yet the delivery of this long-awaited information was enough to cause the vice president of sales to jump to his feet and exclaim "Finally!"

It is important not to oversimplify this task. Traditional data access techniques may not always be appropriate; we may have to bend the rules a little. A large chemical division, for example, was resisting the general manager's request for information on competitive standing. The effort needed to tie into the appropriate databases would delay the EIS introduction, the executives reasoned. Acquisition of this information was rescheduled for a second or third enhancement.

The youngest member of the development team suggested that they just key the data in manually. The rest of the team patiently explained that such a practice was not "maintainable in the long run," that it would create more problems than it would solve. Yet the junior member was right.

There is a strong IS tendency to gravitate toward "architecturally sound" solutions to most problems. Many such executive-level issues are quite volatile, as recognized by our next CW. Still, we often hold onto the rules of the past. Sometimes the low-tech solution is appropriate.

THE PROTOTYPE PROCESS

Most IS professionals are well aware of the benefits of prototyping, regularly modifying the application design with input from the user. Would I argue *against* executive involvement and change? Not exactly, but the trick is in the execution.

> *CW*—EIS must be developed as a prototype, reflecting the ever-changing needs of the executive user.

> *Application*—Do not worry about getting it right; get it quickly. The EIS can be evolved over time, with refinements as circumstances dictate.

> *Implications*—Some developers take this as a mandate to request the executive's regular involvement. Familiarity can breed contempt, and this approach can wear thin very fast. A far more important implication, however, is that prototyping, for many, leads to an enhancement mentality. We improve the content, but we do not change it.

> *Consequences*—My wife's grandmother used to say, "People don't get better, they just get more." This need not be true of people, and it need not apply to EIS. Too often it does. The second iteration of EIS refines the first. We provide more detail, more analysis, more graphics. What we rarely do is offer fundamentally new categories of information.

Maybe this is so because incrementalism is the path of least resistance. Perhaps we want to merely leverage off our existing investment. Whatever the reason, too many executive information systems never grow beyond their initial scope. If this is the result of prototyping, it represents prototyping at its worst.

THE BIG PICTURE, THE SMALL VIEW

Several years ago I was asked to meet with a company's senior officer and "talk some sense into her." It seemed that against the EIS team's good advice, she insisted on seeing large amounts of detail. They were almost apologetic at her "unexecutive-like" behavior.

CW—The executive view is the big picture view. Executives are "Big picture people." They neither need nor in most cases want detail. Aggregations are the building blocks of an EIS.

Application—Develop systems that shield the user from detail. Only provide summary information. Not wanting to turn executives into "analysts," we develop systems well suited to low volumes of data. The technology we select will be well suited to presenting aggregation. This approach increases the distance between the executive user and detailed information.

Implications—Sometimes aggregate data is all we need. What we sometimes forget is this is application- and situation-dependent. On some occasions only the micro view will provide the insight needed for us to take action. Ben Heineman, former CEO of Northwest Airlines pointed out, "There is a huge advantage to the CEO to get his hands dirty in the data because the answers to many significant questions are found in the detail."

Consequences—The EIS may come to be viewed as a toy, lacking applicability to real-world problems. This can result in frustration for all concerned. An executive who relies on the system may make less-than-optimum decisions. Executives who go outside the EIS may be accused of resisting technology or, worse, being "unexecutive-like."

The concept of aggregation is a good idea gone bad. There is an appropriate level of detail to every application and circumstance, but this level should not be dictated by the EIS. These systems should enable the executive process, not inhibit it.

THE SPONSOR ADDICTION

If there were Ten Commandments of EIS, the commandment that "Thou must have an executive sponsor" would be one of the first. This is not surprising. Nearly every major EIS "success" includes the existence of a sponsor as a contributing factor. Furthermore, many of the "nonsuccesses" list the lack of a sponsor as contributing to the project's demise. Many organizations misapply this CW, and another great myth is born.

> *CW*—Do not attempt an EIS project without a sponsor in hand.

> *Application*—For many, this is the same sort of catch-22 they endured while job hunting for the first time: no job without experience, but how do they expect you to get experience without a job? If I should not initiate an EIS without a sponsor, how do I get a sponsor interested without an EIS to show?

> *Implications*—Without an EIS, most take one of two approaches—conceptual or experiential. The conceptual approach is to talk about the benefits of an EIS, to share articles and stories about competitors. The experiential technique is to show the executive an EIS, from a vendor, from another organization, or perhaps developed by your own staff.

> *Consequences*—Rarely will anything the executive sees directly relate to his or her own needs. Sometimes executives can make the connection; often they cannot. If not, it is highly probable that the executive will see the system as nice, but irrelevant. Even if he or she sees a relationship, the EIS may not have the right content to generate sufficient excitement to produce a sponsor.

If you are fortunate enough to have a sponsor, that is great. If you need to cultivate one, however, the best approach may be to interview the high-potential candidates. The content discusion alone may be sufficient to raise the level of enthusiasm necessary. If not, a "sample" EIS would most likely be far more successful based on that content.

CRISIS MANAGEMENT AS AN EIS

In the eternal search for ways to avoid the executive interview, a new twist has been added. If you *really* want to know what interests an executive, identify a crisis with which she or he is struggling. Report on its status, and you will have smooth sailing.

> *CW*—An issue-based approach to content is a good alternative to interviews.

Application—Many view the process of interviewing the executive as not worth the high-visibility risk. They reason that the best way to ensure success is to identify a critical, hot issue. Issues can range from factory fires to strikes, from a hostile takeover attempt to a spill of toxic waste. Deliver status reports and progress toward the issue's resolution through your new EIS, and you will have achieved executive interest.

Implications—The CW of the issue-based EIS is absolutely true, and absolutely false: true—hot issues are by definition of great interest; False—it does not follow, however, that the EIS is necessarily the appropriate mechanism by which to deliver this information.

If this type of content methodology is to make sense, it must pass the test of added value. Is executive effectiveness enhanced by EIS delivery? If the item is truly hot, the executive may be far more comfortable getting verbal updates. Is executive leadership enhanced? Rarely does crisis management enhance one's ability to lead an organization. If the issue-based EIS enhances neither effectiveness nor leadership, then why deliver it?

Even if the issue passes this first hurdle, is it of sufficient added value to warrant the EIS investment? This is not a question of the importance of the issue, but of the added value of EIS delivery of the issue. Remember that many of these issues are relatively short-lived. The EIS investment may persist well after the issue is resolved.

Remember also that an organization that finds itself in constant crisis most likely will find the crises are symptoms of pressing stategic problems. Tangential support of crisis management might be an option to consider, but the well-executed strategic agenda still becomes primary.

Finally, anyone considering building an issue-based EIS should ask what level of executive is responsible for crisis management? Senior managers are often satisfied to receive periodic verbal updates. Lower level management may be responsible for the issue's tracking and resolution. In other words, this could be the right solution for the wrong person.

Consequences—The delivery of status reports and progress toward resolution *may* be a valuable part of a robust EIS. Top management will rarely find this to be of sufficient value to justify EIS implementation and support. At best you may find yourself back to zero; at worst, presiding over the latest white elephant.

THE UTILITARIAN VIEW

In a utilitarian world, function is everything; form is irrelevant. If something has no place in a purely rational world, it should not exist. This is the attitude that decries advertising as pandering to our irrational side. It seems to bother people holding this view not so much that advertisers pander, but that humans have an irrational side.

> *CW*—It has a great personality! The content is everything; appearance is inconsequential.

> *Application*—Some industry pundits take shots at the trend toward touch screen systems (just touch your finger to what you want to see) and top-level graphics. Their argument is that such interface niceties may seem important at first, but quickly diminish in value after several months. The utilitarian view holds that investment in content is wise, but spending on the user interface is frivolous.

> *Implications*—We have all heard of or experienced the blind date who was described as "having a great personality." Long-term, we acknowledge that good looks are skin-deep. Short term, we may develop a sudden headache, and never keep the date.
> Properly defined, great content may be sufficient to keep us using an EIS. That same content, however, may not be enough to propel executives beyond their noncomputer inertia. Attractive screens and an intuitive, nonfrustrating interface are not sufficient to hold our interest, but can go a long way toward attracting the resistant executive.

> *Consequences*—Not everyone backs out of blind dates, and the extra investment in attractive interfaces will not benefit everyone. We are interested in the executive at the margin, the individual who might not be inclined toward the new technology. The utilitarian view may just disenfranchise the very individual who would most benefit from an EIS.

PROTOTYPE, PROTOTYPE, PROTOTYPE

It seems that one of the wost-kept secrets in EIS is that the key to building successful systems is to prototype. EIS, in fact, is sometimes described as the never-ending prototype. This universal truth does have its limits.

CW—The EIS is a prototype. Some people try to get their EIS as perfect as possible before delivering it to the executive user. This delays delivery and frustrates the executive. Ironically, the system will improve most through a process of use and modification; so the desire for perfection actually delays its progress.

Application—Many interpret the CW to mean get *something* to the executive as fast as possible. The highest-priority information is that which is easy and plentiful. Other, higher-value information will come in time. After all, is that not what prototyping is all about?

Implications—Many systems start out well-intentioned, expected to grow in diverse and significant ways. Instead, many just "get more." They grow vertically. They add detail and enhance the vertical perspective, but do not evolve into a qualitatively better system.

Consequences—If the EIS is filled with what is easy and plentiful at its inception, the chances are it will be financial-information intensive, and historically oriented. This meets the need for quick delivery, but places the highest priority on the information that has the lowest added value.

   The EIS should constantly evolve, and speed of delivery is vital to its success. Certainly, there are strict limits to our willingness to delay a project for the perfect content. We need to temper our desire for speed with the recognition that added value at the inception will set the tone for all future enhancements. You can use the principle of prototyping, and still ensure that your EIS gets *better* instead of just "more."

part II
for the
implementers

5

The Implementation Team

The proper selection of the implementation team is far more important than many people acknowledge. Its critical function goes beyond the mere technical. It can expedite development and smooth political waters. Approaching the EIS as a merely technical issue of the right knowledge placed in the right spot, however, there is every reason for one to expect the team to create a technically excellent system that will not be used.

First of all, the "team" is not a team in the traditional sense, but rather a collaboration of four distinct roles. A particular role may not be filled by any one person. The roles are descriptions of activities and the type of person best suited to those activities. For some teams, two roles may be filled by the same person. For others, several people may divide up the responsibility.

These roles should be viewed as complementary to the functional needs of the EIS, and the selected technology's ability to meet those needs. If your organization requires the EIS to support e-mail (electronic mail), and your selected technology does not easily support this, then the team had better be prepared to take up the slack. Each role has its own place in the complementary positioning.

THE EXECUTIVE

The executive's role in the EIS team is not as visible as the three others, but it is just as active a role. Every executive who receives an EIS is in effect a team member, with his or her level of participation increasing with the degree of customization of the EIS.

Some executives seem to enjoy a very active role in the EIS project. They will regularly suggest changes and provide feedback. Others prefer a far more passive role. Participation seems to vary with the nature of the individual. The team should anticipate that executives may wish to participate, and should provide them the opportunity.

Typically one or two members of the team are sponsors of the project. They provide the initial support, help to run roadblocks, and act as a friendly user of the system's first release. Early in the EIS lifecycle, getting a sponsor was not an issue for many of the pioneering organizations. Many of the first sponsors intuitively understood the value of EIS, and were quick to embrace the new technology.

Now that these systems have existed for a few years, getting a sponsor may not be so easy. The early adopters have taken the plunge; the remaining ones are still waiting for evidence that this is a good idea. Because it can take years to document such evidence (there is still debate on the wisdom of CASE, for example), it may be several more years before the next natural wave of sponsors appears.

As we mentioned during the discussion on interviewing, the lack of a natural sponsor need not be an obstacle. The challenge is to help the potential sponsor understand the value of the technology. Interviews, references, and executive presentations can go a long way toward cultivating an executive sponsor.

THE INFORMATION PROVIDER

The information provider is the person who is currently responsible for providing information to the executive. These people are most often business professionals: sales analysts, marketing managers, financial supervisors. Their primary qualification is that they understand their own area function, and they have an appreciation for how the executive wants to look at information.

As the provider will most likely be interfacing with the executive, it is also helpful if she or he can converse at the executive's level. Information providers should have an understanding of the business language peculiar to the specific organization, but most important is their understanding of the business.

The preceding discussion assumes that the organization is building a nonorganizational EIS. An organizational system is a standardized information delivery system, and because it is not designed to customize the information, the need for business understanding on the part of the provider is much less than in the former case. Under these circumstances, it might be possible (or even preferable) to centralize the provider function. This would raise the system's integrity and eliminate the need for the business specialist to participate in a project in which he or she cannot contribute.

Beyond the technical skills detailed here, the provider needs to be a good communicator, especially an active listener. We described the skills necessary for a good interviewer. The closer the information provider can come to this ideal, the better we can expect him or her to perform.

THE ADMINISTRATOR

The administrator is the bridge between the business and the technical world, and the administrator's responsibilities are vital and varied. Among the most important are:

- *Security*—The level of security required by the EIS varies by organization, application, and executive. The administrator is responsible for maintaining that level of security.

- *Integrity*—Once information is delivered to the providers, the administrator can no longer be responsible for the data's integrity. Prior to that point, and for information that may not pass through an information provider, the administrator must ensure that the information is consistent.

    Notice that the administrator cannot ensure that the information is correct, only that it is consistent. The degree to which it is correct is determined by its business, not technical, content. Information can be consistent with the general ledger, for example, but still be wrong. The administrator can only attest to consistency.

- *Logical connectivity*—A single data source feeding an EIS poses little connectivity challenge for the administrator. As the number and types of data sources increase, understanding where to find the right data, the appropriate level of timeliness, and how the different sources combine becomes quite a challenge. Again, this becomes the domain of the administrator.

In addition to these responsibilities, the administrator is often the person who upholds standards, such as implementation procedures, screen and report standards, documentation, and so on.

THE TECHNICIAN

Virtually every commercial EIS available today has a seamy, ugly side. This is the side of the system you very rarely get to completely understand until it is purchased. It is there, and it is waiting for you.

A thorough evaluation of technology will prepare you for not only its existence but also its nature. Home-grown systems, for example, may have components that are excellent by themselves, but are notoriously weak in integration. Some products require considerable programming expertise when one is creating reports, whereas others demand communication skills. The real challenge is not the specific area of technical weakness, but in matching the strength of the technician to that weakness.

No one is technically proficient in all areas. That is why the proper match is so important. If the selected technology is weak in several areas, the team may consist of several part-time technicians, each with his or her own special skills.

There are real limits to dividing up this function. Because each technical area can interact with another, it is all too easy for technicians to conflict—they lose the total picture. Another challenge in using several technicians is that their timing may not synchronize. When one is ready to hand off a piece, the next in line may not be available. This difficulty can unnecessarily delay the EIS project.

THE INVISIBLE TEAM MEMBER

Often there is a fifth member of the team—the consultant. I have seen no statistics on what percentage of EIS projects use consultants, but can safely say that their use is increasing. More and more vendors are including consultancy in their software offerings. Is this reliance on outside consultants a good idea?

There are several reasons for using outside assistance:

- *Timing*—Often there is quite a bit of time-pressure to deliver a system, especially at the early stages of implementation. Many teams consist of "borrowed" resources, many of whom can disappear just as quickly as they became available. It is a combination of tight timing, few resources and high expectations that can make an offer of trained assistance very tempting.

- *Experience*—Many of us will implement only one EIS in a lifetime. Despite the best resources (including books on the subject), there will still be a great deal of trial-and-error learning. Many of the consultants available today in EIS have had experience with numerous systems. They can not only contribute directly to your progress, but can also act as valuable tutors.

  To get the most out of consultants, we should work side by side with them, using this opportunity to learn as we go. Avoid the temptation to assign them some work and let them do it alone. This approach is expedient in the short-term but will ultimately haunt you.

- *Visibility*—Some aspects of EIS are highly visible. This is why the thought of conducting an executive interview scares so many people. If we all begin with trial and error, even selecting our sponsor as the first interview subject can be unsettling.

  Watching an expert conduct an interview can give you the confidence you need to conduct them yourself. You can see how they handle concerns, and how they fill the need for a active listener. "And," as someone once explained, "when they screw up, you have someone else to blame."

There are a few caveats when working with consultants. Remember, this is *your* project. You need to call the shots. You may feel that your approach is better than theirs. This is fine. Clearly they should match your needs. It makes little sense arguing for hours on what you believe to be true. Your career may be on the line, not theirs. Take control.

During the pre-evaluation stages, take care with those consultants who are aligned with a specific technology. They may be excellent at what they do, but their bias can greatly skew the results of the project. During this period you are much better off with a nonaligned consultant.

During the post-evaluation stages, the advice is reversed. Now you are far better able to select a consultant who understands the subtle aspects of the technology you have selected. The application development part of the project suggests that, for efficiency and effectiveness, you make sure that the consultant is closely aligned with your designated product.

CONCLUDING THOUGHTS

While it is fairly obvious where in the organization to draw most team members from, I often get questions about the administrator. Is this person better recruited from MIS or from the user community? Actually, the administrator can come from either place. Our main concern is people-related skills, with technical competency of secondary importance.

Finally, remember that the selection of the team should be driven by the post-evaluation technical needs. This suggests that the implementation team not be selected before the technology. That approach minimizes your chances of matching skills to needs. You may want to consider an interim, first phase team for the pre-evaluation work. This arrangement offers another advantage, in that it affords you the opportunity to view the individual's performance prior to his or her selection as final team member.

The place in the organization that would most likely attract the best candidates is the information center (if one exists). This is the place where all end users go for support. The IC staff is used to working with business professionals and the IS community, and therefore can serve as an excellent go-between.

$\overline{\underline{6}}$

An EIS Chronology

I am often asked about the chronology of the EIS process. This is not surprising. The confusing array of available advice is always presented without consideration of time. Yet even good advice, well-executed, can fail badly if not delivered at the appropriate moment.

With this in mind, we will present a recommended chronology for EIS, taking you from planning, to evaluation, to implementation, and finally to tracking. This is not the only chronology that will work, although it has been designed to economize on resources (including time) while maximizing results. Any variation on this theme is acceptable, as long as you can justify it in your individual circumstances.

The following steps assume only that you have a serious interest in executive computing, and that you have at least begun the process of constructing an EIS team. It assumes that you have neither a sponsor nor committed resources. If either of these is present, so much the better. It is highly recommended that you still include every step.

STEP I: INTERVIEW THE EXECUTIVE

In an early episode of "The Honeymooners," Alice tells Ralph that she wants to work, and that they should hire a maid to do the housework and cooking. "We can't afford a maid!" he bellows; "We can't even afford you!" Logic wins out. Ralph would have greatly preferred to have the money *before* hiring the maid, but recognized that they first had to take the step that would enable the rest of the process.

Many people are surprised and uncomfortable with the executive interview as a first step. There are several steps that seem to have been omitted. But as in our "Honeymooners" example, the first step needs to be the one that enables the rest of the process.

If you lack a clear sponsor, interviewing likely executives will help to sell the concept and identify critical needs. If your plan is to demonstrate the technology to generate excitement, remember that a customized demonstration is many times more effective than off-the-shelf solutions. The best way to ensure relevance is to interview.

You may already have an executive sponsor. So much the better. Remember, though, that your sponsor may not fully (or even partially) understand EIS. It is becoming increasingly common for a senior executive to tell the MIS director, "Get me one of those!," Your chance of success with the project is greatly enhanced if the executive understands what "one of those" is and what benefits it might deliver.

I sometimes am asked how one can get to interview the executive without first creating an EIS? How do you get the executive interested enough to work with you? Try the obvious approach. Say that you are preparing a study to identify the most important information to deliver to executives, and that you require one hour of his or her time. Few executives will say no.

If you cannot get permission for an interview, then you can always charge ahead to the next step. If your senior executives do not think it in their best interests to discuss their information needs with you, however, any further effort on your part may be ill-advised. Either way, you are ready for the next step.

STEP II: ESTABLISH YOUR VISION

What do you want your EIS to be? What would a successful system look like? How would it be used? What benefits would it enjoy? It is important to answer questions such as these *before* you move to any other step. The answers are found both in the interview results and in your own set of objectives.

There is an old comedy album called "The First Nine Months Are the Hardest." In one of the skits, prospective parents are having a tough time selecting a name for their baby. They begin to fantasize about what the child will be like. The husband envisions a boy who likes frogs, goes to parties, and beats up bullies. The wife describes a son who picks flowers for his mother and stays home Saturday night to do his homework. Finally the husband declares, "No wonder we can't agree on a name . . . we're talking about two different kids!" A common vision in defining, selecting, and building an EIS is no less important than this.

STEP III: REVIEW YOUR FUNCTIONAL REQUIREMENTS

What do you want your EIS to be? What are your objectives for the project, what is its scope, and what are your resource constraints? We do not necessarily include financial resources here, as they may remain unknown prior to a formal project proposal. The available headcount, technical resources, skill inventory, and nontechnical constraints are all among the resources to be considered.

Many people take issue with the inclusion of headcount at this time. They reason that, like financial resources, this item must wait for the formal proposal. My experience is that most organizations experience considerable variability of available funds, but follow fairly strict norms regarding headcount. Ask yourself how many people you reasonably think you could get for this project, and use that number as a base.

STEP IV: CREATE THE EIS PROPOSAL

No matter how well-conceived or how brilliant your EIS design, no real progress can come until you get executive approval for the project. With an increasingly large array of inexpensive technology options, some people think they can avoid making a formal proposal to senior management. This is absolutely untrue. The purpose behind the EIS proposal is less financial commitment than it is intellectual and emotional commitment.

Properly executed, the EIS proposal helps us solidify support. By destroying old myths, it also can help us to minimize resistance from otherwise technophobic executives. Lastly, it can provide an excellent early indicator of management's acceptance of the idea. Add to this the financial commitment we often *must* get, and you will understand why everyone should include the EIS proposal in project plans.

STEP V: DERIVE YOUR TECHNICAL NEEDS

Your technical needs will be driven by your functional requirements and expected support. It makes little sense to draw up lists of technology features without this consideration, as these items cannot be prioritized or even included without your fully weighing how they relate to a vision of the project and the challenges it will face.

This evaluation will help you to sort out those needs that are nonnegotiable and those that are frills. It will help you make tradeoffs, and to price the consequences of those tradeoffs. This is especially important when we consider the increasingly wide array of options the prospective buyer faces in the EIS marketplace.

What if you are thinking of building an EIS rather than purchasing one? This is certainly an option, but be careful not to let the tail wag the dog. A surprising number of people tell me they want to develop an EIS product *without* having developed a functional profile. How can they possibly understand what features to include or omit, and evaluate the implications of such a decision? If you are considering making your EIS, your decision process should be no different from that followed by someone evaluating commercial offerings.

STEP VI: EVALUATE YOUR TECHNOLOGICAL OPTIONS

There is an abundance of technological choices available today, and the abundance of options will only increase over the next few years. Organizations can (and do) spend more time and money evaluating the technologies than the price of the technology itself.

This situation is even more ironic when we realize that confusion seems to *increase* with the time spent evaluating options. That is, the more time we spend evaluating the technology, the less difference we perceive. There are significant differences between the technology alternatives. Furthermore, these differences are not very difficult to identify. In short, selecting the right technology for your needs can be a relatively straightforward process.

STEP VII: BUILD YOUR SYSTEM

There are plenty of role models on which you can base your EIS design. Unfortunately, they are mostly minor permutations of the same fundamental paradigm. Their lack of uniqueness does not make them wrong, but it might make them quite inappropriate for your individual needs.

Specifically, there are standards that have evolved around the basic design that do more damage than good (see Chapter 13). Because these standards are so omnipresent, they often appear obvious, logical, and right. There are alternatives, however. These alternatives can offer enhanced productivity and effectiveness—and are just as right for you, as later chapters will show.

7

Deciding What Information to Deliver

The objective of an EIS is to target the organization's information flow to the specific needs of the executive. You would expect it then naturally to follow that the executive would always play a central role in the early stages of defining and implementing these systems. Paradoxically, despite the logic of this assumption, many executive information systems are implemented without any significant executive participation.

The implementation staff may offer several apparently compelling reasons for excluding the executive from EIS content definition. Among the most common:

- The implementation staff understands information requirements as well as the executive.

- It is important to get *something* to the executive as quickly as possible. The content can easily be refined over time.

- We can identify a key project or problem, and then build a system to track and report on progress toward its resolution.

We will examine these reasons one at a time, and then will consider their drawbacks.

1. *The staff knows the requirements as well as the executive.* Under this rationale, directors, managers, and analysts are interviewed to gain insight into those reports and special requests that represent the current executive priorities.

Executive assistants and possibly secretaries also are included in the process in an attempt to capture glimpses of the thought process of the executive. Armed with a log of information crossing the executive's desk for one month, the project team has collected enough raw material to fill two systems.

2. *Get something to the executive as quickly as possible; the information content can easily be refined over time.* This approach falls under the banner of "Gee, isn't technology wonderful!" Providing the appeal of color, graphics, and an easy-to-use system becomes the highest priority. The implementors assume that emphasizing form over content will increase the likelihood of initial executive acceptance.

And the truth is that often they are right. Many executives are exhilarated at the idea of being part of the computer revolution. They often discover that their productivity does indeed increase a bit with the ease of report retrieval.

Finally, the speed with which systems like this are constructed is a refreshing contrast to the traditional MIS application development cycle. It thus is neither surprising nor unusual for an early EIS to be viewed as successful, regardless of the incremental value of the information it delivers.

In the longer run, however, the problem with both of the above approaches is that neither significantly enhances the content of the information being delivered to the executive. Some executives realize this quickly. Others may remain quite pleased with their EIS for well over a year. Eventually, however, many echo the feeling expressed by one CFO: "I prepare my board report in half the time it used to take . . . but it really has not made any impact on how I run or view my business."

Attempts to "evolve" the information over time typically are no more successful than this. Evolution often occurs vertically, adding detail at the expense of adding a broader perspective. For example, the EIS that starts by presenting only financial reporting may grow to include manufacturing variance analysis, but it rarely evolves into a competitive benchmark report. The sales reporting system may eventually include product and regional breakdowns, but may never provide insight into gaps in customer service. The reality is that each incremental investment in added detail delivers a diminishing return in executive value.

3. *Identify a key project or issue; then build a system to track and report on progress toward its resolution.* This philosophy is a pendulum swing

away from the "form over content" approach. Proponents of an issue-based EIS maintain that content is of primary importance, and the hotter the content, the better the EIS. Inventory realignments, reorganizations, critical turnover hurdles, and customer service roblems become potential subjects for an executive information system. Finally, because these hot issues are so well understood at lower levels of the organization, they require minimal executive involvement in EIS content development.

There is nothing inherently bad about issue-based EIS development. Properly selected, this information can be of high impact to both the executive and the rest of the organization. The question is not whether the information is of high impact, but whether the delivery of it through the EIS can add enough value to justify the development effort. There is no question of the importance of critical issue reporting. The importance of the content, however, is not automatically conferred upon the delivery mechanism.

In London, for example, the government had identified the need to transport the elderly to grocery stores, medical checkups, and so on. Their solution was to use ambulances for this purpose. After several years, government officials realized that the same objective could be accomplished much more cheaply merely by using vans. Similarly, selecting critical projects and problems as the primary information content may be seen as too little value for so much resource, especially after the subject crisis has passed. The question is not whether the system will be used, but rather whether EIS-based delivery provides the best added value. Often the answer is no.

DIRECT INVOLVEMENT

The common denominator of the approaches mentioned earlier is that none includes the executive directly in defining EIS information content. Years of experience have convinced me that such exclusion is unproductive in the short term and unjustifiable in the long term.

Every executive understands his or her business. That is not a problem. In fact, the executive's understanding is broader than the more focused views of others who may participate in the EIS. The challenge is to help the executive translate that business understanding into articulated information requirements.

This challenge is not completely unique to the application development world. Those developers who have worked on creating expert systems (computer systems that think like experts) have often reported their frustration with a similar translation problem: trying to get experts (physicians, scientists, and even other system designers) to communicate their expertise systematically. An expert's thought process can become almost unconscious; therefore, the more expert the individual is in the particular field, the greater the difficulty in communicating his or her expertise. For an information systems professional, executives may be just as difficult to interview productively as other subject matter experts can be.

At every conference, seminar, and talk in which I participate, I hear stories of unsuccessful executive interviews. Either very little information was generated, or the added value of what was generated was seen as minimal. Sometimes the storytellers blame the executive, but more often they blame the interviewer.

Having had an unsuccessful interview, survivors often tell others to avoid direct executive involvement in the early development stage. That is unfortunate because that advice influences people in favor of one of the indirect methods already described, with their built-in limitations.

Direct executive involvement in defining EIS content does work. It is, in fact, the only viable method of ensuring that the EIS will reach its strategic potential. The problems that can arise are not inherently due to the personality or the competence of either the executive or the interviewer, but to the way the interview is conducted. Having executive involvement in defining EIS content is so important that the issue should not be whether to involve the executive directly, but how.

The pioneering work in executive interviewing was done by John F. Rockart at MIT. In "Chief Executives Define Their Own Data Needs" (*Harvard Business Review,* March 1979), Dr. Rockart noted that one popular method of direct involvement involved group consensus. Collect the target group of executives together in one room, according to this method, and ask them to agree on what information is most important to the organization.

The problem with this approach is that forcing group agreement brings the results down to the lowest common denominator. Based on this process, groups defined executive information needs no different from the existing reports they had been receiving for years.

The real value of direct executive involvement, as Dr. Rockart pointed out, is in identifying specific information requirements for individual executives. This cannot be accomplished in a group setting.

The purpose of the individual executive interview is to discover what information is most important to the individual executive. It is easy for a first-time interviewer to evaluate whatever the executive says in terms of, yes, that information is reported in existing systems now, or, no, it is not available now. This attitude interferes with the process of getting good information from the executive.

The interview's success should be judged against the breadth of information categories found to be critical to the executive, which should include:

- Mandated reporting (both statutory and internal reporting)
- Operational and financial control
- Management reporting
- Staffing and leadership data

In most companies, the greatest unmet needs for information are in the management and leadership categories.

PRIOR TO THE INTERVIEW

It is quite natural for an executive to want to be prepared prior to any meeting. The interview is no different. You will no doubt feel obligated to provide as much information as possible to the prospective interviewees. *Resist that temptation.*

The executive interview is one time when preparation will likely kill the quality of the meeting. Providing the questions in advance will rarely if ever improve the meeting. To understand why, consider the possible outcomes of such preparation:

- *Passing the questions to the staff*—This is a common method of preparing for a meeting. An executive will, upon receipt of the questions, distribute them to his or her support staff for "input." They will research the questions, and will provide an appropriate response. The executive then may proceed in one of two ways. Sometimes the executive will direct you to the support staff for your material, or alternatively will send the results of their research to you. This all seems quite efficient. After all, you get the answers to your questions, without requiring a meeting. Alternatively, after the executive has received the results of the research, your meeting may consist of the executive's merely feeding you those results. Senior management participation will be only peripheral. In neither case does an interview actually occur, but just the passing of information.

- *Personally preparing for the interview*—This can be quite deceptive, but just as fatal to the interview results. Here the executive personally prepares for the meeting by reviewing his or her information requirements. The "interview" becomes nothing more than a predetermined time to exchange information.

During an interview engagement, I insist that my clients never provide the interview questions in advance. Many feel quite uncomfortable with this requirement. Their discomfort only increases when an executive's secretary contacts them insisting that the questions be provided prior to the meeting. To fully appreciate the danger here, consider an interview I recently conducted for a midwestern consumer goods company.

One of the vice presidents personally called my client (director of MIS) requesting the interview questions in advance. Not accustomed to saying no to this person, the client provided the questions. Two weeks later we walked into the office of a "prepared" executive.

On his desk literally stood an eighteen-inch pile of papers. I eyed them suspiciously, but tried not to be paranoid. I asked the first question, and the floodgates opened! Page after page, report after report, the executive continued his tour of existing reporting. Often he would merely pick up a report, glance at it, and, with a look of disgust, merely say, "And, of course, there's this one." We did finally get to complete the interview, but with only fifteen minutes left to cover the most important information.

Remember that, beyond selling, the purpose of the interview is to draw on the *executive's* perspective of his or her information requirements, unencumbered by existing reporting. There is little that preparation can do to enhance that objective. True, there is always the possibility that some piece of useful information may otherwise slip through the cracks. But this prospect is far outweighed by the damage likely to occur.

What should an executive receive? You will find in Appendix B a list of EIS articles. Many provide overviews of the concept, and contain industry-specific references. Select one, and send it to your prospective interviewee. Some of my clients include a particularly attractive vendor brochure as well. Your cover letter should state that the purpose of the session is to identify that information most critical to the executive's performance, and that of the highest added-value.

If you get the dreaded request for more information, or even the questions, respond by repeating the purpose of the session, and explain that any preparation can only damage the objective. If pressed, hold your ground. I have never had an interview canceled because my client refused to help the executive prepare. If still pressed for preparation, tell the executive that you will be reviewing existing information priorities, *but spending no more than ten minutes* on this topic. At least that way you have a chance for damage control.

THE INTERVIEW'S STRUCTURE

If possible, plan to carry out the executive interview in two one-hour sessions, with the second scheduled several days after the first. Structure the first interview to identify a wide array of potential information needs while minimizing use of the executive's time. As Dr. Rockart recommended, the objective of the first session is to identify as many types of critical information as possible. The second session explores ways to quantify the critical information, as well as potential sources for it.

The sessions typically consist of the executive, an interviewer, who is often from information systems at a level related to the EIS team, and possibly a third person to act as a second set of ears for the interviewer.

The interviewer asks two sets of questions, each designed to explore different areas of the executive's information requirements. These two categories of questions are designed to identify the executive's critical success factors and critical failure factors:

- *Critical Success Factors (CSFs)*—Popularly introduced in 1973, CSFs reflect the business factors most critical to the success of the executive and the organization.

- *Critical Failure Factors (CFFs)*—Complementing CSFs, CFFs are the factors whose existence or lack of existence can contribute to failure. In short, CFFs are an individual's and an organization's pressure points.

THE INTERVIEW RESULTS

The interview process is not effortless. The best interviews are provocative, stretching all of the participants. One executive recently commented: "This is the best hour I've spent in a long time. But I'm glad I get a break before our next session." For the interviewer, the hour is equally intense.

The interview investment should pay off in specific results. Although all sessions are different, most result in identifying information belonging to the following four categories:

- Existing priority information
- Enhancements to existing information
- Unmet operational requirements
- Unmet strategic requirements

Upon completion of this chapter, you may want to examine the sample interview notes found in Appendix A. They should help you to better apply the concepts covered in this section.

Existing Priority Information

Information the executive receives now that has proved to be of greatest value, existing Priority information should be viewed as the minimum content deliverable through the EIS. Without this data, the EIS would be considered incomplete.

Care should be taken in evaluating this category of information. Although its inclusion is required, it adds little to the value of executives' overall delivered information because they already receive this content in adequate detail and scope. The value of EIS delivery in this instance is in the increased ease of access and the appeal of electronically delivered reporting. This data alone does not provide enough added value to warrant the investment in EIS development.

Enhancements to Existing Information

Additional detail on topics that are now being reported, enhancements to existing information set a level of expectation among the executive's support staff. Designing an EIS to include this category gives new direction and incentive to persons currently responsible for supplying information to the executive team (information providers), helping them to justify their effort in adding these specific enhancements to information they already report.

Because most of this information is not being generated by existing systems in a timely or consistent manner, it represents significant added value to the executive, enabling him or her to better control and manage the organization's resources.

These two categories of information, existing priority information and enhancements to existing information, consist predominantly of "hard data," data that is relatively easy to define, measure, and deliver. For that reason, these categories often dominate the content of initial EIS implementations. Because they do not usually contribute much added-value information in the areas of management and leadership, exclusive reliance on hard data can actually cause more harm than good; it does not move the EIS up the scale of perceived value, compared to the existing reporting system.

The following two categories often contain the highest-priority information, which ironically, also is the information that is hardest to get. Because it is not historically based, this information has not automatically grown as a by-product of the basic accounting systems. Much of the information in these categories is soft data, difficult to define and measure in a traditional sense; so it has never been included in traditional MIS development plans. Finally, management's view of information has been shaped (and limited) by years of traditional, hard data. In effect, management has been trained not to demand information in the following categories through the traditional systems channels.

Unmet Operational Requirements

Although much of this information is hard, control-oriented data, it usually has not grown as a by-product of historical requirements and priorities. As information and systems typically develop incrementally, this class of data gets overlooked. For example, in an insurance company, it might include agent productivity. In retailing, there might be a lack of regular reporting of distributor returns.

Unmet operational requirements may be as important than the previous two categories, despite its consistent invisibility in the IS development backlog. In fact, it can be viewed as relatively more important because the other two categories merely add to the information already being delivered.

Unmet Strategic Requirements

This is usually the most invisible of the four categories. It addresses issues that have not yet become crises, but which the executive recognizes as key to the organization's success in the medium term. Much of today's unmet strategic requirements will be tomorrow's unmet operational requirements. These strategic issues often reflect critical management concerns that may not have been formally communicated or even understood as information issues.

Included in this category is feedback concerning the organization's progress toward new destinations. This feedback not only measures executive leadership performance, but, more important, it sends a clear message to the organization about those destinations. Quality, customer service, and cycle time sensitivity all fit into this category.

Unmet strategic requirements are a barometer of the turbulence an executive expects over the next few years. The more dramatic the change expected, the more vital it is that the organization not just react, but that it anticipate that change.

Unless that vision is clear, shared, and visceral, the organization acts as if it is "business as usual," while the executive's frustration will only increase. In a recent issue of *Forbes*, Roger Smith, then CEO of General Motors, lamented the difficulty of changing the direction of GM. He noted that *he* had a vision, but it just was not shared with the rest of the organization. Sharing the vision is one of the more significant benefits of EIS.

THE INTERVIEW QUESTIONS

There are certain interview questions that I use during most sessions. Depending on the progress of your sessions, you may need to either modify these or to add a few more. These few questions will almost always require your full interview time; so do not be concerned about running short.

As you review these questions, remember that the order in which they are asked is very important. They are designed to move the discussion from the easy to the hard, and the order can dramatically impact the pacing of the interview.

1. *What information do you currently receive that is important to you?* In some ways, this is a throwaway question, an icebreaker. It is easy to answer, but often produces answers that are only of marginal interest. When you consider that this is the *only* question many interviewers ask, it is no wonder that people have had lackluster results from interviewing.

It is a good idea to qualify the word "information" in asking your questions. Most people think of information as something that is computer-generated. This can seriously limit the scope of the session. Be sure the executive understands that you mean *any* information, whether received by phone or given on the back of a cocktail napkin. You can decide at a later time whether the responses are appropriate to your EIS requirements. Be careful not to prefilter.

2. *Assume that you have been on vacation for the past few weeks—away from the phone, the office. When you arrive back Monday morning, what are the first things you want to know?* This question was first introduced by Dr. John Rockart as an example of a CSF question. It overlaps some-

what with the first question, but often produces some fresh insight. At the very least, this question helps to prioritize the response from the first.

3. *If you could enhance the information you now receive—improve its value to you—what would you want to change?* Some executives want more detail; others want less. Some like graphics; others prefer more tabular information. The answers to this question are typically all over the map.

The advantage of this question is that it is often quite easy to answer. Often you can significantly enhance the usefulness of information with little effort merely by delivering it through the EIS. This provides a big, quick hit, with very little effort. Just do not acknowledge how easy it will be; save a little glory for yourself.

These first three questions will help to identify existing priorities as well as enhancements to existing information. They rarely address the last two categories of unmet information requirements. These categories are covered by the following questions.

4. *Imagine that you pick up a copy of the* Harvard Business Review *three years from today. You read about our organization, and about yourself in particular. It talks about how well things are going. What does it say?* This question is designed to highlight new directions and strategic initiatives. It deals with the very core of professional survival.

You many find that the executive asks you to repeat the question. Do not be thrown by this. It is a lot to grasp. It is not uncommon for an executive to lean back, place her hands behind her head, gaze up at the ceiling and say "Wow, that is a good question." It is rare indeed for this question to have no impact. More important, it always provides a response qualitatively different from any of the previous questions.

5. *You pick up the same* HBR *article, also three years from today. Now it talks about why things are not going well. What does it say?* You would think that this question would elicit the same response as the previous question, only reversed. My experience is that at least twenty-five percent of the time a new issue will appear. The question is almost always worth asking.

When asking the two *HBR* questions, you may wish to make small modifications. Sometimes it is appropriate to either extend or slightly shorten the three-year time horizon. Other times you may wish to substitute magazines. An IS executive, for example, may relate better to the *Sloan Management Review* (more technical) or *CIO* (Chief Information Officer) magazine. What is important is that the periodical concentrates on strategic issues, and that the executive can relate to it.

Once an executive responded to my *HBR* question by maintaining that *he* would not be mentioned, only his people. His modesty was commendable, but it prevented us from identifying those issues personally important to him. After several efforts, we moved on to the next question. We collected some good information, but to this day I believe that we would have done better had we been able to personalize this issue. (Do not be concerned; this only happened once.)

6. *Envision a specific competitor, and your counterpart at that organization. Imagine you have ten minutes in his or her office. No one will walk in; no one will know. What kind of information would you most like to collect?* Oddly, although I may have a hard time articulating what information is important in my business, I may not have a problem identifying the same thing about a competitor. Often, what I want to know about my competitor's business, I also want to know of mine.

Expect that this question may not make a hit every time. It is designed to help cover the bases. Sometimes the response may be that "I know everything I need to know about my competitors." In that case, just acknowledge it, and continue.

Once, when I asked this question, the CFO stood up and declared the interview over. Thinking quickly, I shot back, "I beg your pardon?" "The interview is *over*," he repeated; "this is an unethical discussion, and I will not participate." I assured him that we were only speaking hypothetically, and that I was not advocating industrial spying. My assurances notwithstanding, the interview *was* over. Fortunately, this happened only once out of hundreds of interviews.

7. *What would you least like your competitor to gather about your business?* This question has the same reverse logic as the *HBR* question. Ask it, see if something new comes up, and then move on.

If you are in the public sector, the issue of competition may not hit home. Try to come up with your own variation on the question. When addressing a session on excellence in leadership in government at Brookings Institute, for example, I asked this question as, "What would you least like the Senate Oversight Committee to know about your business?"—an immediate hit.

8. *Select an organization you admire, one that you consider excellent in some way. What would you want to know about that organization?* We are looking for topics, not specifics, but the latter will naturally emerge during the discussion. If executives respond that they would like to know how that organization achieves high customer satisfaction, then this becomes a critical factor for your EIS.

9. *Over the past several years, have you ever been surprised?* This is a good concluding question. It is short, is direct, and frequently elicits an interesting response. Surprise is caused by our inability to anticipate the future. The intent of this question is to help the executive better anticipate through the use of information.

Expect responses to this question to be all over the map. In every case, however, the issue being addressed will be personally important to the executive, and will relate directly to his or her performance.

WHY A SECOND INTERVIEW?

If all the executive's information needs were of the "hard" variety, there might not be a need for a second interview. This session, remember, is targeted with finding measurements and sources for the information identified as critical in the first interview. Because hard data is by definition readily identified and measured, there would be little sense in committing to any additional time if hard data were the only concern.

Assuming that the first interview is successful, however, a significant number of identified critical factors will be of the soft variety. Many rarely show up in the formal reporting structure, and some have never been explicitly discussed. The challenge of the second interview is to find ways to measure what has never been measured before.

During an interview with the CEO of a manufacturing company based in the southern United States, he bluntly told me that the single most critical failure factor was to avoid "a strike like the one that ripped us apart last year." "What are you going to do," he laughed, "use this system to tell me strike potential every month?" That is precisely what we did do, and to this day it remains his most valued EIS application. On the other hand, if we had decided on our own to deliver the same information and simply presented it to him without any involvement on his part, he would have dismissed the idea as absurd, and moved on to other matters. With direct involvement in the EIS definition process, he was part of the solution and prepared for it.

How do you measure those "soft" factors? Often it helps first to identify the reflective indicators, those factors whose existence suggests the desired condition. A large retail company, for example, wanted to become more innovative. Not surprisingly, there were no measures of innovation to report. This is an excellent example of a soft factor.

Our second interview started with a discussion of the measures of success in innovation. By reporting the outcome of innovation, we obtained a report card on performance, but we recognized that this information was not enough. We wanted not only to know how innovative the organization was, but also how it performed in encouraging and fostering an innovative atmosphere.

This is an important point. If I use information to report on results, I am producing a control mechanism, reactive at best. If, on the other hand, information is provided on the organization's ability to produce results, I am anticipating the future, not merely reporting on the past. The CEO of the retail company decided he wanted not only to receive information on results, but to anticipate those results as well.

We discussed those factors that might indicate a potential to innovate, that would reflect an innovative atmosphere. A partial list of our reflective indicators included:

- Cross-discipline training
- Classes taken outside of one's discipline
- The number of suggestions in the suggestion box
- The number of ideas submitted by customers
- Willingness to take risks

Some of this information already existed. For example, they had always *read* the suggestions in the suggestion box, but never counted them. On the other hand, cross-discipline training had always been encouraged, but never measured. Willingness to take risks had no existing indicators at all.

Quickly our discussion moved toward identifying measures for willingness to take risks, perhaps the softest of the items. How could we measure risk-taking? By counting both successes and failures. How could we count them? By giving awards for both. Suddenly we had a way not only to anticipate innovation, but to encourage it as well. This is the leadership value of EIS.

Quite often the delivery of soft measures can produce some significant surprises. Although this organization had always encouraged cross-discipline training, budget cuts and downsizing over the last few years had actually encouraged management to emphasize specialty performance. Employees were being rewarded and promoted on the basis of technical excellence (specializing) rather than broadening their experience base. This gap was not only highlighted by the EIS, but the CEO was able to set objectives and track progress in the same way.

Sometimes the second interview does nothing more than expand on the first. Often it is an opportunity to identify and begin measuring entirely new areas of importance. It always requires flexibility and creativity on the interviewer's part, and is undoubtedly the most demanding and the most enjoyable part of the interview process.

8

Establishing the Vision

Having conducted the interviews, you should have a good idea of the potential of the EIS. Now comes the hard decision—what do you *want* it to be? This is not a simple question. Fortunately, its answer, although thought-intensive, need not be time-consuming.

There are many different types of EIS. A brief listing of the more popular ones includes:

- *Operational executive*—operational information delivered to a select few executives. These systems are usually control- and/or productivity-oriented.

   Systems that deliver headcount, financial performance, or production statistics to the "executive team" would fit the category of the operational executive.

- *Operational management*—also operational information, but intended for widespread usage. Usually these systems penetrate at least three levels down into the organization.

- *Informational*—designed to help empower employees by delivering information to large groups. Here the term EIS relates to the delivery of information to persons generally believed to be computer illiterate. This might include a "sales EIS," a system designed to deliver critical information to the sales force.

The thing that distinguishes the informational EIS from other types is not just that a large group of people access the information. That can exist for many types. The content of the informational EIS is defined by and targeted to that large group. With this type of information flow, they become primary, not merely a secondary consumer of information.

- *Issue-based*—designed to satisfy the informational needs surrounding a single, pressing issue. Issue-based systems usually are designed around a single executive, but may penetrate fairly deep into his or her chain of command.

- *Strategic*—although it usually includes operational information, an EIS that is targeted to lead the organization into the future, rather than merely monitor the past.

If you are serious about selecting the best technological match to your needs, you should regard the creation of a vision as critical. As we will see, the types of EIS all demand significantly different solutions. Without a clear vision, you are playing Russian roulette with the EIS project.

Can you evolve into your vision? If you believe some of the common wisdom espoused today, the answer is yes. In the late 1980s planners tried to start with an operational EIS. Many fully expected evolution to other forms over time. Conceptually, it seemed like a good idea.

Today we are hearing of the benefits of starting with an issue-based system. It is easier to sell to the organization, simpler to define, and lacks many of the data problems of larger-scope solutions. Again, conceptually it sounds quite compelling.

Let us (for the moment) cease consideration of the wisdom of this sort of evolution. By what standard to you slice through the technological potpourri? Do you purchase (or build) that technology best-suited to issue-based delivery, or that which better meets the needs of a strategic system? My experience is that less than five percent of all evaluations even consider the issue of matching technology to vision (and I might be quite generous with that estimate). The very few that pose the question almost invariably decide on the application most pressing at the time when the EIS is introduced.

What is the net result of the evolutionary paradigm? We select a technology appropriate to the short term, and then are surprised when we are unable to achieve a higher level of evolution. Naturally, this approach is not identified as the problem. We blame the "poor" technology, or lament the unwillingness of management to ante up more headcount or funding. Sometimes we ridicule management's lack of vision, and console ourselves with knowledge that we were ahead of our time. But the consequence of a visionless EIS is almost always failure.

You may believe that technology is application-independent. Certainly if this is true, then the creation of an EIS vision is inconsequential to the application—nice but irrelevant. One of the fundamental themes of this book is that vision and technology are integrally related, that a decision on one will invariably affect the other.

The connection between vision and technology will be explored in the discussion on technology evaluation. If you find yourself skeptical about this issue, you may wish to skip ahead to that chapter. Assuming that you accept the linkage, we can continue.

Although there are many ways to approach the EIS vision process, perhaps the most direct deals with the consideration of a series of questions directed three years into the future:

1. Based on the interview results, what should our single, overriding objective be? To put it another way, how will we know if we are successful?

2. What kind of penetration into the organization do we anticipate? Consider both horizontal and vertical penetration.

3. What will the executives say about the system?

4. How will the EIS be used? This includes frequency and duration of usage.

5. What major events do we see occurring over the next few years? How might these events impact and be impacted by the EIS?

You could certainly add to these questions. Their intent is to ensure that everyone understands what the EIS is targeted to become over the next few years. It is not important that your articulated vision actually materialize. Many things can change during the years, any one of which can dramatically impact the system's evolution. A dynamic system is natural and proper.

We cannot hope to control the future. That is not the intent of establishing a vision. We can, however, shape our future. To do this we need to plan for where we want to be, and how we will get there. Omit the vision, and long term success is virtually impossible.

9

Reviewing Your Functional Requirements

Your vision describes how your EIS will be used in broad terms. With this knowledge you are best able to select the type of EIS that most closely fits your needs. The functional specification fills in the details.

Can you define your functional requirements without first establishing a vision? Certainly, and many organizations do just that. The danger is that the functional requirements will lack cohesion. Some requirements may in fact be mutually exclusive. The value of defining a vision is that it defines your organization's computing paradigm. Within this paradigm, tradeoffs and conflicts are far easier to resolve. The outline of the EIS will already have been drawn. All that remains is to color it in with your functional specifications.

One of the best ways of defining your functional requirements is to respond to a series of questions that portray how it will evolve. Most of these questions require two responses: one for the first six months and another for the next three years. The response for the first six months details your needs during the important launch phase of the EIS. That for the next three years tries to focus your attention on the care and feeding of a successful system.

Why bother to split your response both ways? Most organizations never engage in such a time-oriented discussion. By its omission, however, they tend to be heavily oriented to the highly visible first six months. That might be sufficient if you do not think that your functional needs will change much beyond the launch phase. Probably your needs will change significantly with success, however; so a short-term planning horizon can lead to long-term failure.

Why not just define your long-term needs? Would this approach avoid the short-term horizon trap? Yes, but it would in turn lead us to another trap, just as lethal—farsightedness. Just as someone who is farsighted cannot see near images clearly, excessive emphasis on long-term success may result in decisions that short-circuit more immediate success.

For example, in one company, quick access to human resource information was seen as critical to the success of an organizational development (OD) program. It was believed to be essential to the long-term viability of the organization. Detailed tracking of the sales of a new product could have little long-term impact, but it was of significant importance to the sales group that year. There is no easy answer to managing this tradeoff. Often the ultimate decision is more political than one based on either resource or technical issues. By engaging in this short-term/long-term discussion, however, we ensure that we are operating with full awareness of the consequences—there are no surprises.

WHAT *NOT* TO DO

Information centers (IC) are organized pockets of support for end-user computing. During the 1980s ICs became extremely popular. Most lacked an articulated vision, and virtually all lacked a coordinated long-range plan. The IC sense of mission rarely extended beyond the vague notion of supporting end-user computing.

The results were quite predictable. Support and technology were determined either without regard to functional need or based strictly upon short-term need. The initial burst of success was followed by disillusionment and failure. The explosive growth of users began to outstrip the ability of ICs to support them. Many of the software and hardware "solutions" were fast becoming obstacles. The functional needs of increasingly sophisticated users were not being satisfied. In fact, after a few years, the end-user population had experienced both qualitative and quantitative changes so dramatic that it no longer resembled the group the information center was initially chartered to support.

How did the ICs change during this incredible evolution? In many cases they had essentially the same support staff, software, hardware, training and structure. Many blamed (and still blame) management for lack of financing and inadequate staffing. Yet this ignores the fundamental issue: most ICs lacked a vision or neither articulated nor implemented a long-term strategy to match their vision, and they selected technology independent of any long-term functional need.

Not all information centers failed. Some not only have survived, but have actually thrived during this period. They were flexible enough to change course, and their management was supportive enough to fund their new direction. These are the exceptions that prove the rule. We need an EIS implementation plan, and the starting point for this plan is the definition of our functional requirements.

THE FUNCTIONAL REQUIREMENTS PROFILE

When we speak of functional requirements, we are addressing the nontechnical needs. Figure 9-1 summarizes ten questions fundamental to defining those requirements. As you become familiar with the questions and the issues they raise, you may need to add to these ten. Feel free to do so, with one caveat: simplicity is better than complexity. Our goal is to describe the *critical minimum* requirements, the critical failure factors relating to the EIS's contribution to your business. Less is better than more.

1. *How many EIS users are you anticipating?* This question assumes that the project is successful. Some people have trouble with this question, stating that the answer is hard to predict. We are *not predicting,* we are planning. We will see that the answer will impact both our selection of appropriate technology and our expected support levels.

For some organizations, the answer to this question may be six users in the first six months and six three years out. Another may see the need to grow to two hundred users. Naturally, organizations each will define success differently. It is not important that the answer be correct, specifically. It *is* important that we have a sense of the planned growth over the next few years.

You may want to draw your planned EIS growth curve. This is useful not only in your own planning, but in communicating your plans to executive management.

2. *Would you rate the level of information sophistication of your EIS users as high, medium, or low?* Remember that we are looking at information literacy, not computer literacy. There are six functional needs, each of which expresses another level of insight that the system can provide:

- *Electronic retrieval of reports*—the ability to easily access reports that already exist.

	First Six Months	Three Years Out
1. How many EIS users are you anticipating (assuming the project is successful)?		
2. Would you rate the level of information sophistication of your EIS users as high, medium, or low?		
3. Do you expect a cross-function group of users?		
4. Do you expect a cross-divisional group of users?		
5. Would you rate the diversity of perspectives (report formats) your EIS users will demand as high, medium, or low?		
6. Would you rate the diversity of data your EIS users will demand as high, medium, or low?		
7. What size do you reasonably expect your EIS support staff will be?		
8. List any products you have or will designate as "strategic."		

9. List all possible data sources. Check those for which quick & flexible access might be difficult.

	First Six Months			Three Years Out	

Figure 9-1. Functional requirements profile.

- *Customized reporting*—modifying existing reports to add meaning unique to the individual executive. This includes such abilities as color-coded exceptions and drill down.

- *Exploration*—not just modification of existing reports, but the ability actually to create perspectives (reports and graphs) that may never have been created before.

  Note that even with exploration, although we are creating insight, we are not creating data. All three levels create insight by allowing the executive to leverage his or her business understanding against data that *already exists*.

- *Variance analysis*—the ability to contrast relationships between existing pieces of information, and create new data. Notice that sometimes the need for variance information can be anticipated, and thus built into existing reports. Often the need for variance analysis varies with the conditions reflected by the reports themselves.

  This category can also include trending and averaging. It reflects the need to create new data without materially affecting the existing data.

- *What-if analysis*—evaluating the impact of one change upon another. This might include such questions as "What if our market share increased three percent?" or "How would a headcount reduction impact costs?" Unlike variance analysis, the executive is not only creating new data in this analysis, but is directly manipulating the existing data as well.

  Some persons would protest that their executives (or any "true" executive) would never want to do this. Perhaps they are right. Let us remember that some executives are more quantitatively oriented, more detail-oriented than others. Some might want to "play around" with the data without launching formal studies. Still others might want to consider the impact of policy decisions without sending signals throughout the organization. Use caution when employing the word "never."

- *Computer modeling*—the function that offers the greatest level of insight, by providing the executive the greatest opportunity to leverage his or her understanding of the business. Here the executive not only manipulates the data, but the very relationships (rules) upon which the data is based.

The question of information sophistication is meant to be descriptive.

We are detailing not what we think the individual executive *should* do, but rather what he or she might *want* to do. Some executives are active LOTUS 1-2-3 users, and are in fact using computer modeling today. It is not our purpose to pass judgment on this practice, but to register the need that it reflects.

This is important! In recognizing a functional need (either today or in three years), we are not endorsing that need. We are likewise not establishing that need as a technical requirement of the EIS. Rarely will all needs be satisfied with an EIS. Often the technology and/or the limits of our price elasticity preclude the satisfaction of specific functional requirements. We either cannot do it with today's technology, or just are not willing to pay the price. It is vital to recognize all relevant functional requirements independent of our willingness and/or ability to satisfy the need.

3. *Do you expect a cross-functional group of users?* Is this a "sales" EIS, or perhaps a "financial" EIS? If so, the answer is yes. Often a group will state that the system will start with sales, but hopefully migrate to other functional groups. This indeed may occur, but remember that any migration is predicated on the first success.

The acid test is to ask yourself how success and failure will be defined. If you develop a successful financial system, but it fails to migrate beyond that single-function group, will you still have satisfied your vision? Will the project still be seen as successful? If the answer is no, then consider your needs cross-functional three years out, but single-function within the first six months.

4. *Do you expect a cross-divisional group of users?* Use a logic similar to that of the previous question. It is not unusual to describe our short-term need as divisional and our long-term need as cross-divisional. Continue to ask yourself, "If we only delivered this level of functionality over this time frame, would the project still be considered a success?" If the answer is no, then redefine the long-term requirement.

5. *Would you rate the diversity of perspectives (report formats) your EIS users will demand as high, medium, or low?* Some organizations want their EIS to support a single, standard view of the business. That may in fact be a major motivation for the EIS project. If that is the case, you might respond that users want low diversity, both short- and long-term.

Often the three options—high, medium, or low—are overly simplistic. You may believe that some executives will *never* want more than standard reports, but others will demand highly customized perspectives *today*. Again, use the same acid test question detailed above: If we only delivered this level of functionality over this time frame, would the project still be considered a "success"? This critical failure factor approach should help you to take a position.

6. *Would you rate the diversity of data your EIS users will demand as high, medium, or low?* Naturally, this question directly relates to the clarity of your vision. If you are unclear about the business needs the EIS will address, you will find your answer to this question likewise vague.

Notice that this question on data diversity is different from that of divisional or perspective diversity. One financial EIS might deal exclusively with financial perform ance reporting, and therefore have low diversity of data. Another financial EIS, however, may require data from human resources, purchasing, manufacturing, and logistics.

Remember also that we are building a profile based upon our best assumptions at a point in time. Reality can, and most certainly will, differ from those assumptions. From a relative perspective, we are still far better off building from those assumptions about the future. The alternative is to merely extrapolate on the basis of history. Although we can quantify history precisely, it is far better to be approximately right than exactly wrong. Your intuitive judgment about the future may be more reliable that a history-based projection.

7. *What size do you reasonably expect your EIS support team to be?* This question is often misunderstood. Many look to the "experts" for this information: "You tell me how big the team *should* be!" Yet that approach begs the business question.

Although the size of teams will vary during the launch of the EIS, the ongoing support team averages about three persons. Such averages can be deceptive. Some organizations employ one full-time person, whereas others commit over twenty people to the system.

Almost everyone involved in an EIS project has some idea as to a team size that would be considered reasonable. You, better than any outside expert, know what will most likely constitute the outer limits of committed headcount, both short- and long-term. It is better to plan for a conservative number and be pleasantly surprised.

You may notice a significant mismatch between the resources you could ever commit to EIS support and the level of requirements you have identified as representing functional needs. Do not worry about the implicit "stretch." That is the value of planning, to highlight any imbalance between objec tives and resources. The way to handle a possible imbalance will be addressed later in this process.

8. *List any products you have designated or will designate as "strategic."* An increasing number of organizations have implicitly or explicitly designated specific software or hardware technologies as strategic. The stra-

tegic designation means that the specific product will be *the* resource for any project requiring related functionality. If MacIntosh is strategic, then all personal computers purchased will be Macs, with very few exceptions. If IBM's DB2 database product is strategic, than it may become *the* repository for all end-user and management data.

The strategic product issue is a functional rather than a technical question because, like the other functional requirements, it becomes the criterion against which all technical solutions will be judged instead of just another feature. It adds another item to our list of critical failure factors: either our EIS interfaces well with our strategic products, or the likelihood of failure increases significantly.

9. *List all possible data sources. Check those for which quick and flexible access might be difficult.* Here we are concerned with identifying possible barriers to success. It is not that these barriers cannot be overcome—they can. But overcoming barriers might require either more resources than planned, or the acquisition of specific technology. Either way, we are much better off identifying such needs early in the planning cycle.

10. *List all critical failure factors.* Beyond those items covered above, what are those factors whose existence (or lack of existence) is likely to cause the EIS project to fall significantly short of its goals?

What might be included in this requirement? Anything is appropriate that you think is critical to *your* organization and executives. For example, you may not have listed your e-mail system as strategic, but believe that any executive system that does not integrate with it will not succeed. For many organizations, extreme ease-of-use is critical. Some companies have executives who are quite computer-literate. For them, computer literacy may not be a critical factor at all.

CONCLUSIONS

Anything that smacks of planning is often seen as postponable—nice, but unnecessary. When you are under pressure to produce results, you often feel so pressured to advance to the "real" activity of evaluation that you skip steps that may appear to be optional. Don't.

Everything builds on the functional requirements. Creating the profile of functional requirements may only take days. Once complete, it can literally save months of misdirected effort. The definition of the functional requirements is the expression of the EIS vision. A well-thought-out profile can make the difference between success, mediocrity, and even failure.

10

Creating the EIS Proposal

Probably half of all EIS projects are officially launched with a project proposal to executive management. Those that are not launched in this way should be. The proposal can be in writing or, preferably, delivered as a presentation. Either way, it should be considered a must when you draft your implementation plans.

REASONS FOR THE PROPOSAL

Why bother with a formal proposal? This is a valid question, especially in light of the increasing numbers of senior executives who are actually instigating the EIS project. Does the proposal become redundant, a case of "preaching to the converted?" The answer is an emphatic no!

There are several compelling reasons to include the formal proposal as a key step in your implementation plan:

- Closing the communication loop
- Reducing resistance to change
- Managing expectations
- Getting the resource commitment

Closing the Communication Loop

Recently I asked to audit the direction and progress of a large EIS development project. The CFO, I was informed, was enthusiastically behind this project. As we were waiting in the atrium of the executive suite, my hosts further elaborated: "He said that he expects this project to be of major importance to our company. No question, he is the ideal sponsor." During our meeting with him, I asked for his impressions of the EIS, emphasizing his expectations of its benefits. "Why, with it we'll be able to project sales over the next few years. We can play what-if games with exchange rates, and model the global economies."

Not surprisingly, my two hosts grew very quiet. Their mouths dropped slightly open, and one came startlingly close to assuming the fetal position. As we left the CFO's office, they finally broke the silence: "What the hell was that?" my near-fetal friend exclaimed. "Where did he ever get the idea that was an EIS? *Maybe* a DSS/Econometric global model, but not an EIS!"

It is very dangerous to underestimate the potential for mixed signals in dealing with senior executives on EIS projects. They are typically very difficult to access, and dialogue is rushed, at best. Further, many potential implementors are so pleased with the support, they are afraid to "look a gift horse in the mouth." For whatever reason, your proposal presents the best opportunity to be sure everyone shares the same base of understanding.

Reducing Resistance to Change

In a typical organization, one-third of the executive team will actively support EIS, one-third will resist it, and two-thirds will remain skeptical about whether it ever will get off the ground. The EIS presentation is designed to detail the many benefits of EIS, but, more fundamentally, to defuse active resistance to the project.

It does not matter whether this resistance is open or covert. It does not even matter that your personal roadblock is not targeted to receive an EIS in the near future. If any executive has the potential to be an impediment to the project, that potential should be recognized and addressed.

I was once asked about my attitude concerning the "organizational jackass" ("You know, the type who won't stop trying to shoot down the project at every opportunity"). I tried to offer the observation that this person might not actually be a jackass. I tried to point out that there could be an honest difference of opinion, but the MIS director would have none of it. "I'll tell you what I'm going to do," he continued; "I'm going to just ignore him, installing an EIS for everyone else. When he sees how successful the others are, he'll come around."

I had not realized that his question was a rhetorical one. He already knew what he wanted to do. His plan was to starve out the recalcitrant VP. He almost chuckled at the thought of this "jackass" crawling to him a year later, lips parched for want of a drop of information to quench his executive thirst. "Tell me," I asked gingerly, "is your 'organizational jackass' a man with clout?" The director clearly had not yet roused from his daydream. I asked whether the man could change from jackass to albatross, and actively become a danger to the project. The director allowed that this was indeed possible. We regrouped, and started to plan some other options.

It is probably not reasonable to expect all executives to embrace the concept of EIS simultaneously. Some, in fact, may never be persuaded to participate. It is unnecessarily dangerous, however, to implement a system with the active resistance of one of the executive team. A major value of the formal proposal is that it can greatly decrease the likelihood of such a problem arising.

Managing Expectations

Software vendors used to have a slogan concerning the risk of overselling: Do not confuse selling with implementation. As frightening as this may sound, it is based on solid sales psychology. One should not expect acceptance of a marriage proposal that is accompanied by confessions of insanity in the family. It follows that if you want the sale, you worry about the "details" of implementation tomorrow.

Few reputable vendors subscribe to that idea today. They have repeatedly discovered that the short term gain is hardly worth the long term damage to their reputation. Many of those who find themselves thrust into the role of "selling" EIS have not had the opportunity to move up that learning curve. They enthusiastically promote the many virtues of executive computing, while minimizing the very real resource commitments and risks that also follow.

Properly designed, the proposal can manage the balance between selling and implementation. It can excite while maintaining realistic expectations. Perhaps most important, everyone hears the same message, minimizing the chance that you might go slightly overboard when dealing on an executive-by-executive basis.

Getting the Resource Commitment

Sooner or later, you will have to "go for the close." Unless your interest is purely educational, you will have to make a case for money, people, and time. Some people prefer to rely solely on a written cost justification to make their case, but there is much merit in introducing resource requirements during the proposal stage.

STRUCTURING THE PRESENTATION

I have been designing and delivering executive presentations for many years. During this time I have observed what does and does not work, both in my presentations and in those of others. Based on this history, I will suggest a structure for your EIS executive presentation. This is not the only format that works, just a particularly successful one.

Many executive presentations are risky at best, doomed to failure at worst. The problem lies in the presentation's objective. It is not that people lack a clear objective when they prepare a presentation, but rather that they do not understand how to match the presentation to the objective. That is the key to proper design.

Common wisdom dictates what a "proper" design is:

- Tell them what you are going to tell them.
- Tell them.
- Tell them what you have told them.

This overly simplistic design is adequate (barely) if your objective is education, but totally inadequate if you need to excite, persuade, and move to action. True, it is a logical design, but successful change management and sales (yes, sales) are less logically centered than emotional and psychological. I am not proposing fact distortion or manipulation. I am suggesting that the structure you use to express these facts can have a very significant role in how they are received.

PRESENTATION PHILOSOPHY

How long should your presentation be? I am regularly appalled to hear of two- and even three-hour executive presentations. Unless your strategy is to "wear the bastards down," I strongly suggest that you consider making your presentation tight and hard-hitting. You want your group to leave pumped up, not worn out. The most import design consideration is independent of content entirely. Ask yourself what the maximum length can be that will still leave energy levels high. Thirty minutes? Forty minutes? If you begin to exceed one hour, start asking the question again!

"In principle," I often hear, "I absolutely agree, but there's no way I can say what I need to say in such a short period of time." Let me reiterate: There is *nothing* more important than a tight, hard hitting presentation. *Nothing*. It is not an issue of how much you want to say, but of how much your audience can hear.

There have been numerous studies on attention span. They all conclude that the average attention span for an adult is approximately twenty minutes. After that, one's attention fades in and out. The longer your presentation, the more frequently you will lose the executive's attention—this is unavoidable. However, you can control (1) the amount of fade-out and (2) where the fade-out will occur.

You control the amount of fade-out by limiting the length of the presentation. A predetermined length becomes your target. To meet the target you will have to work on your pace, prioritize your material, and find creative ways to express the same concepts more succinctly. This takes more work than a less controlled approach, but is well worth the effort.

You control where the fade-out will occur, not by manipulating the executives, but by manipulating your material. The high-impact messages should come early; the exposition, history, and theory should come last. Notice that this is precisely the reverse of the way that most presentations are designed. The norm is to start with the history and exposition, move to the theory, and then "grow" to the climax, the main message—to spend the precious, high attention, first twenty minutes on the lowest-priority material. The climax, then, may very well occur after half the audience has faded out.

Having picked a time target, we are ready to begin designing the presentation. The design I am recommending consists of a multistep process, as explained in the following paragraphs.

DESIGNING THE PRESENTATION

Step 1: Reduce Resistance

There is little sense in presenting your proposal if people in your audience are thinking: "Another song & dance by MIS"; "Great . . . more promises"; "I can't learn to use computers."

Before you open your mouth, before you show your first slide, they will have turned you off. Nothing you say, no matter how strong your case, can have an effect if it is not heard with an open mind. This is always true, but in view of the many computer prejudices held by senior management, it should be axiomatic.

Try starting your presentation by listing some problems with information in your organization. List as many problems as you can. Naturally, you will not connect with every member of your audience every time, but the chances are that each executive will get at least a few major hits. I have had CEOs elbow controllers and say, "Paul, he's been spying on our business," or "Ouch, that one *really* hurts!" The idea is to start out by addressing directly the things that cause frustration. True, they are only symptoms. You will be talking about causes later in the presentation.

Initially, all we want is to start making heads nod. Every executive attending the session should understand from the outset that this presentation, at least potentially, relates to his or her needs. The symptoms should be selected by first constructing a list of all possible problems, using information to which an executive might relate. Any that are not related (directly or indirectly) should be removed.

Step 2: Create Relevance

The first step has already established relevance to the executive. This next step relates the relevant information to the EIS proposal. It accomplishes this by briefly explaining why the symptoms exist.

The explanations should be high-level, and presented in an orderly fashion. I would suggest between five and seven items here. Using too few is simplistic; using too many becomes confusing. Although the list is hardly exhaustive, some commonly mentioned problems include:

- Limitations of paper reporting
- Historical bias of existing data
- Multiple definitions for sales, cost, and so on
- Data access problems
- Getting no added value from information providers
- Time lags inherent in the existing system
- Traditional development methodologies

Each item should make sense in the context in which it will be viewed. The executive should understand, for example, that traditional development methodologies are perfectly appropriate for some applications, and the consequences of such approaches are inevitable for those applications. The next step, of course, is to show that EIS is not one of *those applications*.

Step 3: Introduce the EIS

Only now that the executives have a paradigm through which they can understand their current plight can we begin to introduce the EIS. Even here we avoid a purely logical introduction to the topic, however.

Start out by briefly describing the attributes of the EIS, following closely with a discussion of its benefits. These benefits should relate to cause and effect. For example: "We use a powerful, very fast development approach (vs. traditional methodologies). This reduces response time, minimizes programming, and makes modification easier. We can become very responsive, delivering your first system within six weeks, and many modifications within 24 hours."

Depending on the expected skepticism of your audience, you may consider supporting all or some benefit statements with independent verification (press stories, other user stories). The primary goal here is to help the executive appreciate the potential benefits of the technology, relative to the symptoms with which you opened your presentation. The emphasis needs to be that "This is *why* you cannot view this project from the same old paradigm."

Step 4: Personalize the Benefits

Many of the symptoms listed at the beginning of your session related to all the executives, without regard to their circumstances. The benefits thus would follow the line of productivity and efficiency. To address benefits to the executives' careers and the organization, your points also should highlight critical business issues.

For example, how might the EIS impact employee crosstalk, quality programs, and increasing globalization? What could it add to increased competitiveness, employee empowerment, and the need for greater innovation? These suggestions are not meant to offer a shotgun approach to benefits. Each item discussed should firmly strike a chord with a specific executive.

To personalize the benefits is to begin talking business issues, not just computing. You should choose the benefits selectively, citing examples of such applications. The use of references is not mandatory, but goes a long way to persuading executives of the validity of your case.

Step 5: Explain the EIS

This is a brief description of how the EIS works. It is very important for your coverage not to get excessively detailed. Few executives will want to understand the technology, but most will need to appreciate the project's scope. Are you replacing the general ledger? Building a new sales database? Eliminating all paper reports? Remember that what is obvious to you may be a real concern to someone in your audience.

Step 6: Present Resource Requirements

You have made your case. Your audience should now appreciate that many of their most frustrating problems with information can be reduced by fundamentally changing the paradigm of traditional reporting. You have provided evidence of the benefits they might expect, and added enough detail to convince them that it is not experimental, and does not require smoke and mirrors.

The final step is to explain your implementation plans, including an estimate of resource requirements. These requirements should deal with personnel, time and money. Both the plans and the requirements should be tied to a time line for implementation. Although this aspect can vary, you may want to consider a time line similar to the following simplified illustration:

- First two months Establish EIS team
  Interview selected executives
  Select software and hardware

- Next two months Deliver five systems

- Next six months Interview remaining executives
  Expand and enhance the EIS
  Evaluate effectiveness

- Ongoing Support and enhance the EIS

Your implementation plan should be detailed enough to confirm to the audience that the project is well considered, and that it will be tightly controlled. Your resource requirements should be reasonable, commensurate with the benefits you have specified.

THE PRESENTATION'S CONCLUSION

I have seen little gained in providing a historical retrospective of executive information systems. Likewise, explaining to senior executives that "business is becoming more complex" or "change is happening at an increasingly rapid rate" will not make them more receptive to your case. If, however, you feel compelled to include such discussion, the conclusion is the place for it.

Few executives will be moved by statistical curves showing the growing popularity of these systems, but a carefully placed mention of a competitor's system might get their attention. Remind them of a few of the primary benefits of the system, and your presentation is complete.

Several questions still must be settled:

1. *Should we include a demonstration during the presentation?* A demonstration of the EIS technology can be very effective in making your presentation more tangible. Your audience can decide for themselves whether the system is *truly* easy to use, and the impact of a visual image can be quite exciting.

Extreme care should be taken not to let the technology be the message. If you decide to include a demonstration, it should complement your message, not dominate it. A twenty-minute demonstration of the EIS might be effective, but rarely would a presentation benefit from a forty-five minute show of technology.

2. *How would I structure a demonstration?* The answer to this question varies with the specific situation. Basically, you would want to follow the same principles in a demonstration as with your presentation, concerning attention span, avoidance of technical details, and so on. The emphasis should be less on *what* it does (drill down, color coding) than on *how* executives might use the EIS (investigating more detail, easy identification of exceptions). Above all else, it should be benefit-oriented rather than feature-intensive.

3. *Should an EIS vendor do the demonstration?* This is a difficult question. The vendor will (most likely) be more accomplished at performing demonstrations, so that approach will seem smoother. On the other hand, not all vendors are adept at avoiding feature-based demonstrations, and this drawback could undo the business message of your presentation.

Some vendors will not let you play with their ball unless you let them play too. If you are committed to the demonstration, the question may be moot. In any case, there are some basic points you should insist upon:

- It is your show—their participation is designed by you.

- This is an internal presentation. You will call them into the room at the appropriate time, and they are to leave at the conclusion of the demonstration.

- Their participation does not imply that they are the chosen product. It creates no obligation for either party.

4. *Should the executives be interviewed prior to the presentation?* Under ideal circumstances, interviewing some or all of the targeted executives is a good idea at this point. It lowers the surprise potential of the presentation, and gives you some excellent, relevant material from which to draw benefits. The challenge, however, is to interest the executives sufficiently that they want to spend the time with you. Often this interest is first generated by the presentation.

If you can interview even a few executives participating in the presentation, your position will be enhanced. If not, remember that the presentation approach detailed here has worked time and time again. Prepare thoroughly, manage the process, and you will be successful.

11

Deriving Your Technical Needs

The evaluation of technology that is adequate to meet your EIS requirements is not necessarily complex. If not done properly, however, it can be extremely time-consuming and frustrating. Today the average time that an organization spends on evaluation is six to nine months!

Does that kind of commitment produce the results people are looking for? Ironically, most evaluation teams admit that the more time they spend during this process, the less difference there seems to be among products. Confusion seems to increase in proportion to the time spent.

George Bernard Shaw once received a letter from a famous actress of his time. She suggested that they pool their genes to produce a truly superior child. With her looks and his brains, she reasoned, the child would represent the best of both worlds. "Madame," he responded, "with our luck the child would have my looks and your brains."

Similarly, most corporations seek to "marry" the diverse disciplines of DP professionals and end users in the evaluation process. The typical user understands his or her business needs, but falls short of translating those needs into the appropriate technology. Conversely, the DP professional understands hardware issues and such concepts as data dictionaries, security, and data integrity, but is naive when faced with the critical issues of end-user requirements. Rather than complement each other's strengths, however, such unions, left to their own devices, often just compound each other's weaknesses.

Still other companies purchase $100,000 of software upon reading an advertisement or seeing a demonstration. A few of these firms might even consider the use of the software to be successful. The vast majority of users, however, understand the importance of their EIS purchase, and seek to reflect this in the selection process.

EIS tools are aimed directly at that segment of the corporation most responsible for directing critical resources. Improperly chosen, these tools can drain the very processes they were intended to enhance. The cost of the software is minimal compared to the impact of the selection on the corporation.

There *are* significant differences between many EIS products available today. The solution to performing a successful evaluation lies not in the amount of time spent, but in the approach you take to it.

No evaluation should take more than three months, and many can be effectively completed within six weeks. The first steps (EIS vision and functional needs assessment) were treated in prior chapters. If you skipped over that material with the intent of jumping directly "to the meat," I urge you to return to it. Those chapters lay a critical foundation for a quick and resolute clear evaluation.

UNDERSTANDING FITNESS FOR USE

There is no such thing as perfect software. All software will fall short of your needs in some areas. Nevertheless, some organizations conduct their evaluations as if they are searching for perfection. Further, it is not enough to conduct your evaluation on the premise that you will select the product with the fewest flaws (or greatest technical strengths). To do this ignores the reality that every organization is unique, and that different organizations have different needs.

How do organizations differ? Some are quite technically proficient, with a corresponding high level of computer literacy, even among executives. For them, ease of use has an entirely different meaning than it has in the company whose executives have never touched a keyboard. More to the point, the implications of lower ease of use in the computer-literate organization are quite different than in the many non-computer-literate organizations.

Even "pure technology" must be considered relative to the individual organization's profile. For example, would you consider security an important component of an EIS? Many people think that it is, and spend vast amounts of time agonizing over tradeoffs between security and other important components. This may be appropriate if an organization does not own security software, or if it lacks specific skills in this area. An organization with demonstrated strength in security might not place the same emphasis on security as on an important EIS component.

To be sure that your evaluation matches the needs unique to *your* organization, check the critical failure factors you listed in the section on functional requirements (Chapter 9). If you are lacking strength in any particular area deemed important for EIS success, then this area should be listed as a CFF. Notice that we are not talking about the total absence of software, hardware, or skills. We are trying to discover any factor about which you do not feel confident of success. Only by establishing a complete profile of your organization's functional needs can you hope to assess a particular technology's fitness for use.

WHAT IS WRONG WITH CHECKLISTS?

Many EIS teams approach the evaluation process from the perspective of a checklist. They list features they consider to be components of an EIS and then use this list as a backdrop against which they evaluate a technology's fitness for use. My experience is that use of a checklist rarely (if ever) adds to the evaluation process. There are several reasons for this:

- *The kitchen sink*—The first step in creating the checklist is the list itself. Here there is a tendency to include *everything* that might ever be a factor in EIS, and then add from there. First, there are those items that we identify during our brainstorming sessions. Then we ask the vendors for their suggestions. Finally, we may solicit suggestions from others within the organization, often those deemed "experts."

  Any item contributed by a vendor should be considered suspect. This is not a reflection on the vendor's ethics, but rather a recognition of the vendor's first commandment: "If you can't fix it, *feature it*!" Remember that a particular feature may be critical for one vendor's product, but inappropriate for another's.

  Asking an expert can be no less confusing. A database expert may contribute those criteria "essential" to a good relational database; the data administrator will talk about active data dictionaries and security "musts." We are not, however, trying to select the best database, security package, or communication software. We are simply trying to produce the best fit to our EIS functional requirements.

- *The weighting problem*—We sometimes try to circumvent the problems associated with lists by assigning a weight to each item on the list. We might, for example, assign bar chart graphics a weight of 10, with 3-D bar charts receiving only a 6. Every feature gets a weight. At the end of the list we tally the results. But then what? Is the product with a 220 score *really* ten percent better than the product with 200?

    If a requirement is truly a CFF, then it does not belong on any list. It is not just twice as important as another item, it is required, period. Because weighting puts everything in relative perspective, it masks the CFF's primacy. It is entirely possible for a weighted checklist to point you in absolutely the wrong direction.

- *The environment problem*—Is ease of use important for your EIS? Most people would emphatically say yes. How do you account for this importance when using a checklist? Give it twice the weight of everything else? Three times the weight? That begs the primary issue: how do you evaluate ease of use independent of what is being used?

    Many functional requirements, such as ease of use, cannot be considered independent of what is being used, and by whom. Communications may be a trivial task for one technological solution, but an enormous headache for another. One product may be excellent at producing standardized reports easily, but requires considerable advanced training to allow customization. The limitation to checklists is that they treat every feature as independent, whereas many factors in the EIS (or other high-level technologies) are highly interdependent.

In summary, checklists are rarely limited to those items critical to the EIS. If they were limited to CFFs and CSFs, many of the listed items would be interdependent. There is no easy way to reflect those cross-relationships with a checklist format.

There is nothing wrong with merely *listing* those CFFs and CSFs related to executive information systems. Doing so can help us to consolidate and organize our thoughts. We will see that we can even use these lists to create "checklist" maps that will help us anticipate functional gaps in alternative technologies. However, reliance on checklists to help us compare products' adequacy is almost always a mistake.

EVALUATION PHILOSOPHY

There is no such thing as perfect software. Every technological alternative has flaws. Our purpose in evaluating technologies is not to find perfect software, but to minimize surprise.

We minimize surprise by thoroughly understanding our unique functional requirements, matching the technology's strengths and weaknesses against those requirements, and understanding the short- and long-term implications of that match (or mismatch). If a product seems well suited except for its data acquisition capabilities, I can anticipate that weakness, include the purchase of a third-party software package, and weigh the potential penalty associated with a nonintegrated third-party solution.

The philosophy of minimizing surprise recognizes that every organization has technical and support strengths and weaknesses. These characteristics can become either catalysts or impediments to success. Matching them against a technology's own strengths and weaknesses, we can anticipate where problems will arise. Having done so, we can plan an implementation strategy that maximizes success.

Do not expect a great deal from EIS vendors during your evaluation. They will quite understandably portray their solutions as "perfect" for your needs, while pointing out that the competitor's product will lead to certain failure. Their black-and-white worlds often bear little resemblance to your environment, and therefore can confuse rather than illuminate. The reality is that vendors all have within their ranks organizations that have succeeded wonderfully with their products, and others that have experienced total failure.

What is important is that you have a way of quickly and confidently evaluating the adequacy of any technology, either purchased or homegrown. The evaluation should fit *your* organization. After the evaluation, you should be able to complete your implementation plan.

THE EIS EQUATION[1]

There is a balance, a simplicity, to understanding the basics of EIS technological evaluation. This paradigm is reflected in the following equation:

$$\text{Functionality} = \text{Technology} + \text{Support}$$

The delivered benefits of any EIS solution are a direct result of both the technology and the human support. You need not worry about striking this balance—it will occur quite on its own. In fact, you cannot keep these components from reaching equilibrium. If you manage the equation, it will produce predictable results, with surprise avoided and the chance of success maximized. Thus we see precisely why so many systems fail: rather than manage the equation, we too often tend to concentrate on the pieces.

What is the consequence of imbalance? To understand it, we need to appreciate the interplay of each part.

Functionality. This term embraces the essence of our functional survey. We include all the delivered benefits, integration to strategic products, and anticipated levels of demand, both short- and long-term. This factor is completely variable. We may (and should) know specifically *what* level of functionality we want, but the level that is *actually delivered* after implementation can vary considerably.

Technology. We often think of this category as quite variable. It is not. Once we have committed ourselves to a specific technology, we reduce our flexibility considerably. We become married to specific architectures, specific structural dictates of the technological solution.

An understanding of technology is an understanding of limits. Some of these limits are potentially short-term only. After all, product features come and go. If a specific technology does not support 3-D charts, for example, it would be unreasonable to condemn it on that basis alone. Unless you had a short-term CFF that demanded 3-D charts, you might have a reasonable expectation that it would be supported in the near future. As long as you are confident of the vendor's development strengths, technology features can be treated as truly variable.

Sometimes the limits can be compensated through the use of third party solutions. As long as your selected technology can be integrated with these outside solutions, you can also consider the technology to be variable. The degree of variability is dependent on an open architecture, your cost flexibility, and any perceived loss of ease of use. If there is no resistance to the extra cost and integration is trivial, then again you can consider the technology variable.

All technology has some limits that are genetic. That is, nothing short of a complete rewrite of the software would alter its boundaries. Because the technology's genetics are generally fixed, once committed we are married for life. For this reason we devote our greatest energies to understanding a technology's genetics, and the limits they impose.

Some people are attracted to the home-grown option for the very reasons we have discussed. Because of the "do-it-yourself" approach, they feel they can overcome any limits. They believe the limitations of purchased technology are the result of losing control. "Retain control by building your own system," they reason, "and you guarantee flexibility."

In reality, a home-grown solution is often among the least flexible. Even the most sophisticated solutions are developed as applications, tailored to specific needs. These systems often are ill-prepared for the dramatic swings an EIS can experience.

On balance, we should consider technology as fixed for the short term, and at best semivariable for the long-term.

Support. For most organizations, support is relatively fixed. It is rare to hear of an EIS support team growing from three to ten, for example, but it is not uncommon to hear of an additional person added to the team. To plan conservatively, however, consider the most likely level of support available initially, and treat it as fixed.

What if your implementation plan calls for a *scheduled* increase in headcount? Consider the support growth curve as fixed. If you have approval to start with three and grow to six, then recognize that your support level will not exceed those limits over the given time period.

THE EIS EQUATION AND SUCCESS

How do you measure success of your EIS? Delivering the functional requirements? Certainly that would be considered success in anyone's eyes. But what if you could not deliver all the functionality detailed in your original plan? Would that be considered failure? It would not be if you *anticipated* that shortfall and included the lower level of functional benefits in your final plan.

Success comes not from delivering what you *want* to deliver, but rather delivering that which you have promised. How do you keep from overcommitting? By using the EIS equation to understand the balance, you can understand what can and cannot be provided.

The IS organization for an East Coast retailer presented a persuasive set of EIS benefits to their executive management team. The presentation was successful, and they received approval to spend $60,000 in the creation of an EIS. They purchased the "best product" that fit their budget, and four months later delivered the EIS. It initially was well recieved, but by year's end executive dissatisfaction was surfacing and six months later the project was scrapped.

The VP for information systems blamed management's unwillingness to fund the project sufficiently. However, that was not the problem. Given a $60,000 limit, he never went back to management with a revised set of benefits. Had he done so, they could have increased the funding, accepted the lower functionality, or scrapped the project before it began. Any of these options might have avoided the problems that occurred. His proposal was unbalanced, with predictable results.

Let us take another look at the EIS equation:

$$\text{Functionality} = \text{Technology} + \text{Support}$$

Support, as we discussed, is relatively fixed. We want to treat our desired functionality as also fixed. In reality, we must recognize that if either technology or support does not match our planned levels, our functional requirements will have to be adjusted. Our approach is to start by defining our desired functionality, as well as our expected level of EIS support. With these two components in place, we can try to derive the final component, technology.

COMMON EIS FEATURES

A few features have become industry standards. They rarely are significant issues in the evaluation process because they are shared by many products; but because of their importance to the EIS, we first should examine these standard concepts.

- *Hot spot*—Traditionally, menus of options were offered to computer users in an easily discernible way: they were presented with choices, numbered from one to ten, and then instructed to select one of them. As the number of options increased, however, what once seemed easy became incredibly cumbersome. Sometimes it seemed that the menus outnumbered the information.

  A hot-spot allows the designer to transform the information (traditional display only) into a menu of options. To create a hot-spot, the designer designates specific text, numbers, or any portion of the screen as "pickable," a hot-spot. On touching that spot (with either a touch screen or a mouse), the user is taken to the designated next screen of information.

  Properly designed, the use of hot-spots simplifies the look of the screen, and makes navigating around the EIS a more intuitive experience.

- *Drill down*—Most briefing books are organized in a drill-down approach. The summary information is presented first, with all the supporting detail afterward. With drill down, the user selects a hot-spot and is presented with the next logical level of detail supporting that number.

  The advantage of drill down is that it is a passive presentation of options. Paper reports force the user to move through multiple levels of detail, whether desired or not. If a specific level of detail is desired, the user must again fight the paper medium, sifting through irrelevant detail to find the target information.

- *Exception reporting*—A typical report has thousands, if not tens of thousands, of numbers. Quite often, the first (if not the only) thing an executive wants to see is nonstandard performance—what is unusual. One way of doing this uses exception reporting.

  Exception reporting allows the designer (and sometimes the executive) to specify a specific range of tolerance. If the values on the report are within that range, nothing may happen. If they are out of the range, the numbers are presented in such a way as to highlight the exception.

  There are several ways to indicate out-of-range events through exception reporting. The numbers can blink, change shading, even trigger alarms. The most common technique employs color coding.

- *Color coding*—Colors can provide a powerful means of intuitively communicating important information to an executive. The most common standard is red when the exception is below reasonable performance, green when it is above, and yellow when it is within acceptable limits.

IMPORTANT EVALUATION CONCEPTS

Recently I was asked to help an organization review its IS strategic plan. During our discussion members of the organization mentioned that they had just returned from a two-day overview of a new EIS product that was being released. I skimmed through the product brochure, and then discussed with them the strengths and weaknesses of the product. They said they had come to similar conclusions, but were amazed that I picked up in one minute what had taken them two days. Armed with an understanding of some fundamental concepts, however, anyone can quickly sort through the strengths and weaknesses of individual technologies.

Eight basic areas differentiate technologies:

- Architecture
- Data evolution

- Communication

- Data access

- Information administration

- Hardware

- Resources

- Support

Each differentiating area has its own implications for an EIS. An understanding of these concepts will not only help you in evaluating technologies, but also in folding your technology selection into your implementation plan.

Architecture

One of the starting points for evaluating technologies is to assess their architecture. Understanding its architecture helps us to understand why a technology acts the way it does. There is no single "right" architecture. By understanding the implications of each type, however, you can better determine the best fit to your needs.

Open vs. Closed

No man is an island, and rarely, it seems, is an EIS. Information often comes from a variety of sources, many of which are external to the EIS. The ease with which technologies integrate with these external sources is the distinction between open and closed architectures.

An open architecture (in its pure form) accepts information from every source, regardless of format. Notice that we are referring to information, not just data. Your organization may have a set of LOTUS reports, for example, that have become a standard for executive reports. The open architecture does not require you to re-input that data, nor does it necessitate the re-creation of a report that already exists. It can accept the LOTUS report in its existing form and integrate it into the EIS.

Some technologies are able to accept charts in addition to numeric reports. Still others can accept and display *any* image, regardless of origin. Scanned photographs and images from Harvard Graphics, for example, can become a functioning part of the EIS.

Notice that the fact that an open architecture can *accept* reports in their existing form does not mean that those reports cannot be enhanced. Although some technologies merely allow you to display reports created elsewhere, others provide a good many more options. Often you can add color, headings, hot-spots and exception reporting. This allows you not only to integrate but also to enhance existing reports.

Although there are several major advantages to an open architecture, remember that they do not necessarily provide a benefit to you. Unless you expect that a significant percentage of your information will come from diverse sources, and there is an investment in existing electronic reporting, you may never actually enjoy the advantages, which include:

- *Leveraging the existing investment*—This can lower the support required to write reports for the EIS. It is especially valuable if you have a wide variety of report formats. For example, one application may contain forty significantly different reports. It is a wasteful use of support and resources to create these forty reports again, just to satisfy the architecture of the technology.

- *Data integrity*—Every time a human hand touches information, there is an opportunity for mistakes to be made. If the human hand enhances the information in some way, the exposure may be worth it. If the intervention does not add value, but only duplicates effort, the loss of data integrity can become a significant problem. An open architecture minimizes unnecessary handling of information from external sources, thereby increasing data integrity.

- *Cycle time*—The main way we usually think of time is as it applies to response time: the time between the hitting of a key (or mouse) and the appearance of information. From an executive perspective, this is far too limiting. What is most relevant to an executive is the length of time required to get information.

  With an EIS, we can think of cycle time as the time between the request for information and its delivery. Cycle time is a much broader concept than response time, but when it is slow, it has the same effect as a slow response time. As an executive, when I want information, I want it now. Any significant delay frustrates and irritates me. With enough delay, I may just stop using the system.

  An open architecture can reduce or eliminate the need to create many reports. Thus it can speed delivery of critical information to the executive user, and thereby significantly reduce cycle time.

With such a compelling list of benefits, you may wonder why someone would want a system with a closed architecture. Closed systems offer their own set of advantages, which under some circumstances become benefits to us:

- *Intelligent reporting*—A pure open system understands nothing of the data that is being reported. Every step in preparing reports for consumption requires human intervention. This is not true of a closed system.

    Because a closed system can "own" the data, it can build in some unique understanding of what the data means and its relevance. This understanding can automate some level of reporting, reducing support requirements.

    One way that reduced support shows up is in the generation of basic EIS reports. Say, for example, you have fifty product lines, with a corresponding set of several hundred reports being generated on those lines. If a new product line is introduced, how does it impact support? A pure open architecture system does not distinguish between product line data and any other type. All modifications to existing reports must be done manually. A pure closed-architecture system can recognize that a new product line has been introduced, and automatically reflect that change in all the reports.

- *Data integrity*—Whereas open architecture minimizes the handling of data from *external* sources, a closed architecture system minimizes handling from *internal* data (already captured within the system). In the above example, every one of the reports that requires updating becomes susceptible to error because they require human intervention. Further, the greatest error—that of omission—also can occur. If the provider forgets to make a change, it will not get done.

    Data integrity is in fact one good way of measuring a system's intelligence. Ask the question: "If the source data is correct, and the system is properly designed, can I still get a wrong answer?" If the response is yes, then you are looking at a nonintelligent system. A truly intelligent system guarantees the correctness of its information. It may *allow* the data to be modified by human hands, but it does not *require* such modification.

You will notice that both open and closed architectures can legitimately make claims that *their* solution minimizes support requirements, maximizes integrity, and increases productivity. Depending upon your individual needs and how you apply the technology, both solutions can provide similar benefits. If an architecture is mismatched to a set of needs, however, benefits can be very hard to come by. That is partially why one organization will swear by a particular vendor, and another will swear at the vendor.

One last word on architecture: it rarely exists in its pure form. Many technologies have "borrowed" from each other, forming a composite of both open and closed architectures. With few exceptions you should be able still to discover the technology's architectural genetics. The value of this discussion is not to create a corner that you can paint a technology into. The tag is unimportant; the implications matter. Use your understanding of the implications of open and closed systems to probe for critical weaknesses and strengths.

Data Evolution

Every EIS product now on the market can deliver reports electronically. This is a requirement of the EIS, not a differentiating factor. Virtually every EIS product on the market is capable of displaying static reports. Similarly, most products offer color coding, drill down, and so on, which also will not help us to appreciate significant differences in products.

Electronic delivery of static reports does not add meaning to information; it adds productivity. Information can be viewed more quickly and with increased visibility, but the user will rarely gain new insight. Data evolution deals with the ability to alter the data so that it offers increased insight to the user. Data manipulation represents a first-order improvement in this sophistication, and with it a real increase in insight.

Data manipulation treats a report as a collection of values, which can be presented in a variety of combinations. By reorienting the presentation, we can cull new meaning from the basic report. Although no *new* data is created, data manipulation does allow for a new level of insight.

There are two fundamental limitations of data manipulation. The first addresses the degree of manipulation allowed. Some technologies allow only for column manipulation. Others allow for the swapping of columns and/or the swapping of rows, but not swapping columns for rows. Naturally, the more that the data can be manipulated, the greater the potential for new insight.

The second limitation of data manipulation involves ease of use. It is not at all unusual to hear vendors extol their ability to manipulate any information in virtually any way. They may even demonstrate the incredible ease which they can accomplish manipulation. What is often unstated is that ease of use is inversely related to the degree of manipulation. The more you can do, the harder it gets.

What are the implications of this software sleight of hand? One large bank had planned for a full-time support staff of three people, with a distributed provider network of twenty business professionals. They selected a software package with a demonstrated ability to manipulate large numbers of reports. Their plan was to launch the EIS by delivering a centralized set of 150 primary reports. During the second phase, they reasoned, the providers would manipulate those reports, leveraging off their knowledge of how the executives would most want to see the information presented.

The first phase was quite successful. The second phase, however, was not so fortunate. The providers all required considerable training to learn how to appropriately manipulate the reports. Some were nervous about their computer skills and opted out of the program (saying they were too busy to participate). Others simply thought they could not afford to take the time to learn the new skills. The few who accepted training found that their use of the software was too infrequent to let the training stick. In the end, the EIS career stepping-stone became a tombstone for the three central support staff. They blamed lack of support from "lazy" providers, overly demanding executives, and insufficient funding. The real culprit was the technology.

It is not enough to understand the technical capabilities of a technology. We need to appreciate our own support potential (in both numbers and skill level) and match that with the technology's ability to deliver capabilities to that group at an appropriate level of complexity.

Data Maturation

We saw that data manipulation adds insight to the application, but that manipulation is possible only where the reports already exist. If a report does not exist, there is nothing to manipulate. Data maturation moves data up the evolutionary curve toward greater insight. Whereas manipulation changes the presentation of the report, maturation can create reports that never existed.

What is the value of data maturation? A typical report may contain two hundred data values. Manipulation allows these values to be presented in any number of combinations. Although an improvement over pure delivery of static reports, this is still a fairly small sandbox in which to play.

Contrast this with a database of data values, which might contain two hundred thousand data values. Now we are talking about a big sandbox! The insight potential is tremendous because ninety five percent of the possible reports may never have been created.

Another way to appreciate the distinction between static reporting, manipulation (dynamic reporting), and maturation (unlimited reporting) is through the concept of exploration. All other things being equal, the greater the number of possible perspectives, the greater the potential for exploration, and the lower the potential for frustration.

Some people object to this notion of executive exploration as "turning the executive into an analyst." Although it is true that an analyst may need to explore the business, it does not follow that this is only an analyst's function. Most executives regularly try to explore their business with the aim of identifying potential issues early and querying those responsible. They may not want to *solve* the problem, but they need to uncover it early.

Status reporting is valuable for monitoring and control. It can help to identify problems early, when they are limited to predefined areas. Exploration requires a flexible way to quickly move through many different perspectives of the business, and can rarely be predefined. A status reporting system is not inferior to one that supports exploration; however, it is often inadequate to satisfy the explorative process.

There are some significant limiting factors to data maturation. Most obvious are the sleight-of-hand risks we discussed with manipulation. Because the technology is adding to function, however, the vulnerability to a corresponding increase in complexity is also quite real. At some point we may pay too great a price for the increased capability.

The danger of diminished ease of use is much greater for maturation than for manipulation. The person doing the manipulation, after all, is most often the information provider, for whom ease of use (and ease of learning) can be defined as several hours of training with minimal retention. Maturation (and the exploration it implies) can be accomplished only by the primary user, the executive. As an executive, I need to be the one to do the exploring because I often do not know in advance what I am looking for and want an immediate response. Such browsing cannot be done by anyone other than the executive user, and for the executive, ease of use is defined as ten minutes of training and zero retention. In other words, by jumping from manipulation to exploration, we are greatly enhancing the application's function, without adding to complexity.

Another limiting consideration with maturation is the response time of the system. With each evolutionary step, from static reporting to manipulation and finally to maturation, comes a corresponding increase in processing requirements. All evolutionary steps must contend with system delays stemming from display response time, but processing delays can become a real problem.

What are the implications of a slow response time? In the extreme, it can eliminate an executive's willingness/ability to explore, regardless of the technical capabilities of the system. Exploration is trial and error. We expect that ninety-five percent of everything we view will *not* be of interest. We need to move through the uninteresting material quickly, to support our thought process, and quickly come to the five percent that *is* interesting.

An application's ability to support quick exploration (browsability) is limited by both its ease of use and its processing speed. The paradox is that we often improve ease of use by giving the computer more work to do. This often requires extra processing, which in turn can slow response time. Because the system delays often increase with the demands of browsability, they are not consistent. A technology can demonstrate extraordinary speed when delivering status reports, only to slow to a crawl when shifted into the browse mode.

Data Creation

Every step in information evolution discussed so far has addressed *existing* information. Executives have an enhanced potential for insight when they can see old information in new ways. Some of them may never require more than this.

Many executives have the need to create new data, although they may not be aware of it. Calculating variances on information, for example, is quite common for virtually all management reports. Variance analysis allows us to compare two sets of numbers and evaluate the degree to which they differ. The need for variances sometimes is quite predictable, so that the analysis can be embedded in status reports. This is particularly true of monitoring and control applications. But the need for variance analysis cannot always be predicted.

The lack of predictability extends from status reporting through exploration. In the case of reporting, the status report format may not change from month to month. I can even predict that management will always want to see actual-to-budget variances. A need to see variances for travel expense, however, is context specific. Only when the numbers look "weird," for example, might I want to examine the variance of specific expense categories.

The more exploratory the application need is, the greater the requirement for data creation, the most popular form of data creation being variance analysis—a reflection of this manage-by-exception world. Another useful, although less popular, form of data creation is forecasting, projecting trends from historical information. The projection the executive creates is totally new. The data was not provided, and may not, for that matter, exist anywhere.

Other forms of data creation can include summations, averages, and, in rare situations, statistical analysis. Each act of creation adds value to the application—mostly by telling the user what is not interesting, sometimes hinting at what is. Because the questions an executive may ask are often unique to that individual, data creation allows for customization to a degree not feasible before.

Notice that data creation is important to both the information provider and the executive. The provider is a vital member of the EIS team because she or he can add business perspective to any given application. Without the tools to express this perspective, however, the provider's ability to contribute is greatly diminished. Similarly, the executive also adds value to the application by synergistically combining business experience with the existing information. Data creation leverages both the provider's and the executive's experience in working with the EIS.

One caveat is necessary for employing data creation techniques: be certain the executive user understands the techniques' limitations. This is not a significant issue when dealing with summations and variances. Forecasting techniques and statistical analysis, however, can easily mislead even experienced users. This may be one occasion when a small dose of training may be in order: not necessarily on how to use the capability, but about when to use it, and how to interpret its results.

Data Modification

Whereas data creation allows the executive to *add* data, modification provides the ability to actively *alter* existing values. Examples of the latter include sensitivity analysis (what outcomes would result from a range of changes?) and goal seeking (what input value would provide a target outcome?). The most common example, however, is what-if analysis (what would be the outcome of a given change in input?).

There is no agreement as to whether modification functions such as those mentioned are within the executive purview. Although some members of senior management do use some of these "game-playing" functions, most do not. Before you write off data manipulation as not important to you, remember that to date very few EIS products offer such capabilities. Also, these functions can represent advanced learning hurdles. Even if they are implemented in a user-friendly fashion, they can require a level of information sophistication not *yet* developed by your executives. But what about the future?

Beyond the issues already mentioned, there is one other challenge to data manipulation: integrity. No, I am not speaking of the problem of executives "messing with the data." That can easily be handled by protecting the data from being permanently altered. The challenge has more to do with the possibility that the answer might not match the question. In other words, the executive user might get a wrong answer.

When a user applies data manipulation functions, he or she is activating a rule-based model of the business. If the query does not extend beyond a spreadsheet representation of the business, there is no problem. Virtually all modeling products can handle such requests with one hundred percent integrity. If, however, the query spans a more complex representation of the business, the modeling product needs to be able to automatically reflect the query results, regardless of its impact on other products, divisions or distribution channels. This is quite a difficult problem, one that very few products can adequately address. If data manipulation is important to you, research this issue carefully.

Modeling

For those who are uncomfortable with the concept of an executive manipulating data, the thought of modeling (manipulating rules of computer logic) is positively terrifying. Yet there are some executives who regularly develop LOTUS 1-2-3 models. It is not a question of whether you might consider it appropriate. If that is what your executive expects, not delivering that level of functionality could frustrate and aggravate your senior user. Even if no one wants such capabilities today, what about tomorrow?

Again, it is not important how you feel about this issue. You should discuss and debate the question with your team. Make your team's final position explicit, and proceed with the evaluation on that basis.

One final caveat: beware of the "average user" syndrome. It is reasonable to expect that some executives *today* might want to move quite far along the evolutionary path. Whether information-literate or computer-literate, they will be your most demanding users. Others may never want more than simple delivery of standard reports. The selection of a technology often draws a functional line beyond which you may not proceed. This line can disenfranchise your more demanding users.

As long as your technology selection matches your implementation plan with respect to targeted executives, there is no problem. If you find that you might be excluding some highly desirable executives, you may want to rethink your selection.

Communication

Not all EIS products provide the ability to communicate. An executive user who wants to "reach out and touch someone" had better pick up the phone. The implicit philosophy of this approach is that the purpose of EIS is to deliver information to the executive, not function as a multipurpose workstation. Besides, most executives are "people-oriented." They will not want to use the computer to replace their conversations.

An increasing number of EIS practitioners are discovering the fallacy of the noncommunicating EIS. In 1988, finding an EIS installation that supported communication was very unusual. Two years later, the majority either were currently supporting it or had plans to do so in the near future. Among commercial products, communication capabilities had become the standard.

If communication has become so common, why do we consider it a differentiating factor? We do so because there are still technologies available (including build-your-own) that fail to offer any integrated communication solution. Furthermore, many of the more complete offerings differ significantly in their approach. If this capability is important to you, it warrants close scrutiny.

Data Access

We stated above that the CSF interview process must take place without regard for the "practical" limitations of data availability. Once CSFs have been identified, however, IS is faced with the very real challenge of materializing what was yesterday "vapor-data." Examining EIS products, we find that some exhibit the implicit philosophy of "Give me your data, I'll give you the world." For some organizations, it is not quite that easy. Fortunately, there are some options available.

Foreign File Interface

Reports are the universal language of business, and in working with reports foreign file interface (FFI) provides the safety net of access techniques. It assumes only that data being sought exists somewhere in a report. By "reading" reports, it can provide access to virtually any information that is important to your organization.

Although there are differences in approaches among FFI systems, there are some basic similarities:

- They all read electronic reports, also called flat, fixed-format files. These files, if viewed on the computer, would appear exactly as they do in report form.

- The user of the FFI system uses a computer language (usually fairly simple) to direct the system on how to navigate around the report, and what information to extract as it does. This is usually done with a combination of character strings and column positions.

- The FFI usually puts the extracted data into files in a format readable by the EIS, to be imported into the EIS in a final step.

An advantage of FFI is that it can import into the EIS virtually *any* information, independent of the source. The primary requirements are that the information can exist as an electronic report, and it can be viewed (the technical user has password and hardware access). The fact that the source data is not touched maintains the integrity of the system, and it is not necessary to have the intervention of a database or an application specialist every time new information is requested.

FFI has its downside as well. To briefly summarize some of the issues:

- *Aggregation*—Many FFI systems cannot aggregate. Thus they must rely on the EIS system to perform the aggregation. Because much modeling and relational (and relational-like) software can be relatively resource-intensive, this can cause very real problems, depending of course on the volume of data to be aggregated.

- *Resources*—Many FFI systems are resource-intensive themselves. If the FFI can aggregate, this one capability can offset the efficiency limitation. If the system lacks aggregation, this consideration becomes a much higher priority.

- *Nonintelligence*—Many FFI systems are nonintelligent; that is, they do not handle dynamic changes in the source files. The implication is that the integrity of the entire system may be put in jeopardy.

The variation in FFI systems is quite significant. If you think this capability will be important to you, you may want to closely scrutinize the specifics of the vendor's offering.

Direct Access Trunk Line

Another approach to accessing information outside the EIS is the direct access trunk line (DATL). This differs from the FFI approach because it requires neither an electronic report nor the creation of an interim file of extracted data. DATL allows the technical user to directly view and manipulate the original database itself, but to do so from "within" the EIS environment. If you are interested in pulling data from five different data sources, there is no need to become proficient in each database. Once the desired data is identified, there is no need to create an interim file. The data usually can be imported directly from the target database into the EIS.

The advantages of DATL are that it is usually quicker and much more efficient than FFI. Because it gives the technical user a window into the database, it also provides a level of analysis and query not available with FFI. For these reasons it is often the technique of choice if available.

One potential disadvantage of DATL is that it is often significantly more technical than FFI, limiting the number of technical users qualified in its operation. Because it must be designed for each database it supports, there are only a limited number of data sources that will be satisfied by DATL. Finally, although it is usually more efficient than FFI, it may consume significantly more resources than other, nonintegrated third-party options.

The importance of hostile data access cannot be overemphasized. EIS must be designed around the executives' need for support of their decision process. Lack of attention to data access realities invariably leads to an EIS that is actually little more than electronic delivery of by-product information.

Information Administration

Information administration is concerned with the security, timeliness, and integrity of the information provided to the executive user. There is no function delivered by the administrative capability that cannot also be delivered by human support. When considering the value of information administration (IA), then, you want to consider it less as an independent feature and more in terms of the workload it relieves the support personnel of.

We call this capability information administration because unlike the situation of traditional data administration, here we are primarily dealing with reports, charts, memos, and other chunks of knowledge. Although data falls within this category, it plays a much smaller role than it has in the traditional data administrative function. We need to be keenly aware of these differences when evaluating the EIS because the criterion needs to be quite different from that of traditional approaches.

Resist the temptation to place your data administrative expert in charge of this part of the evaluation. If the two capabilities are confused, the best *data* administrative tool can produce the worst information administration results.

IA is far from being universally important. Its relative value to your organization is directly related to your business profile. The considerations discussed below are especially important.

Organizational vs. Customized EIS

In an organizational EIS the information that is distributed is fairly standardized. Any differences between the executives who are supported are accomplished at the local level by the executives' direct support staff. There is no centralized support for nonstandardized information. A customized EIS, on the other hand, can support any number of executives or a group of executives.

The primary area of IA concern is in delivering a centralized supported, customized EIS. Under these circumstances, we still would use information providers, but their role would be to participate in increasing the customization, not to administer it. Notice also that the IA capability becomes increasingly important as we move closer to having a maintenance-level EIS. This might explain why IA has received so little attention up to now. Expert systems, for example, have been around for several years, but only recently has the maintenance of these systems come under scrutiny. Thus, the majority of EIS installations may only be beginning to deal with the issue of maintenance. Unfortunately, by the time they do, we will have made our technology decision. Our choices on how to bring our EIS into balance are limited—increase the support, decrease the customization, or support fewer executives.

What are the implications of a customized EIS and information administration? Suppose for a moment that you have twenty executives whom you have targeted to ultimately receive an EIS. Some information that they receive will be of universal interest, such as stock price, organizational profitability, revenue, budget performance, safety records, and so on. At the other extreme, personnel profiles, performance evaluations, and confidential memorandums may be exclusively for the use of one individual executive. Between those two extremes, information might be sharable within departments, or between specific executives, executives and their staff, divisions, an so on.

Issue- or crisis-based executive information systems are more in line with the organizational-type EIS, because the basic issue is centralized, a specific issue. Uniqueness of perspective is rarely a concern.

The issue of customization is not limited to *how* an executive wants to see information. Another serious aspect of this issue is that executives are limited as to what they are allowed to see (security). For example, if you are delivering information that is available on an organization-wide basis (perhaps the annual report), security is virtually a nonissue. However, for some types of information, only the most secure EIS will win the executive's trust. If executive users do not believe a system can support the necessary security, then they will most likely not trust their most important information to the system.

The issue of security is not just about the amount of security, but also involves how much for whom. Just as different executive groups and subgroups need to see different subsets of information, security needs also vary with each information subset.

The issue of integrity is one of matching the right information with the right executive. It is not a question of "Is the data correct?" but rather "Is the data appropriate?" Timeliness, for example, can vary significantly from user to user. One of my clients (a corporate controller) insisted on seeing the sales information each day. Ironically, the sales VP believed that daily sales were "not actionable." He only wanted weekly sales figures. The question was not, "Which of these executives was right?" but rather "How do we satisfy the different needs of the executives without undue impact on support?"

Timeliness is not the only consideration, however. With any EIS, data may come from a multitude of sources. Each source has its own sense of timeliness and must integrate into the EIS in a rational manner, with high integrity.

Hardware

Some technologies are dedicated to only one specific hardware platform. As long as you support that platform today, and have no plans of supporting others in the future, then there is no need to pursue this issue any further. An increasing number of organizations, however, have a diverse set of hardware and operating system platforms, and at least several of them may have to be supported. This need can greatly narrow the number of technology options we have. If we only support MacIntosh computers, we can only consider Mac-based solutions. If we expect some of our users to use MacIntosh, and still others IBM, the circle of options is further narrowed to that software running on both platforms.

Be aware that some options are not quite this obvious. One technology, for example, may run very well on IBM's VM operating system, but quite poorly on MVS. Another product may run well on MVS and poorly on DEC hardware. We must recognize that having the hardware and operating system platforms supported by the vendor is merely the first hurdle. The follow-on question becomes: "How well does the software perform in my environment?"

We need to appreciate just how significant these hardware/operating system decisions can be. Members of a midwestern retail chain spent seven months evaluating various software alternatives. After selecting a product, they calculated its cost to be almost $750,000! Its purchase would have required a new mainframe computer and new personal computers for every executive user. They thought they had chosen the best product, and that may have been true. The best product *for them,* however, needed to fit their environmental limitations. In the end they purchased a different product and, by their estimation, had wasted a full six months.

Resources

It is ironic that technology efficiency is evaluated when one is considering an EIS. I have asked people why they think this is, and their opinions seem to differ significantly. One gentleman suggested that it is because resources are not really an issue with EIS. He reasoned that so much of the technology is PC-based that the resources can be regarded as free. This cannot be so because many EIS users find themselves running third-party products to supplement their EIS, primarily because of resource issues. One woman speculated that the level of funding for the EIS was so significant that resources became irrelevant. That also cannot be the whole reason. The question of cost justification seems to be more popular than ever. Further, EIS efficiency and software workarounds are popular topics at most EIS user group and industry conferences. This situation is not indicative of a cost-insensitive market. My own speculation is that we still tend to consider and evaluate an EIS in terms of the information we deliver directly to the PC. From a resource perspective, this is perhaps the least important consideration of all.

What we really need to measure is the incremental impact on our resources of the EIS. This includes data extraction, aggregation, calculation, and any other interim requirements prior to the local delivery of the information.

Also of potential importance is executive usage. Some technologies provide static information viewing via PC delivery. Any exploration on the executive's part may require mainframe resources. Our evaluation thus must include not just resources required to meet our EIS supply require-ments, but also those necessary to satisfy executive demand.

Support

Support obviously is not a feature of EIS technologies, but it is a significant differentiator. We have already spoken to this issue at some length in discussing the EIS equation. In some cases it can be the single most important differentiator in the evaluation.

Remember that when considering support requirements, we need to consider the amount of support, who will be providing that support, and the functionality (business capabilities) the support will provide. As you begin to examine the evaluation process in the next chapter, always ask yourself, "What are the support implications for my organization?" Do that, and you greatly minimize the likelihood of surprise.

REFERENCE

1. I developed the concept of the EIS equation jointly with Linda Applegate, Professor of Business Administration, Harvard University.

12

Evaluating Your Technology Options

This chapter assumes that all the prior steps have been completed. Further, it assumes that you have a sponsor and a commitment of funds and support. Without these requirements in place it is very likely that you will be wasting the time of your team, as well as that of the vendors. If you think you require the assistance of a vendor to help "sell" a sponsor, then select one strictly for this purpose. You gain nothing by putting yourself through the rigors of evaluation until all the pieces are in place.

In search of a "no surprise" selection, we have discussed how some of the more substantial differences in solutions involve deciding between open and closed architectures. To a significant degree, the battle lines have been drawn here. You will need to make other decisions, however, before jumping into the evaluation fray.

One necessary decision is to select the development philosophy your organization will employ. This is critical because most firms implicitly evaluate technologies by using prototyping, a scaled-down version of what they expect to develop. This evaluation approach is only as sound as the development philosophy upon which it is based.

DEVELOPMENT PHILOSOPHIES

Everyone has an opinion, and the younger the discipline is, the greater the likelihood that those opinions will differ significantly. EIS development is no exception. It is not surprising that each opinion has its own compelling logic. What does seem to surprise many people is that selecting a development philosophy that does not complement your own special circumstances is courting disaster. Consider the following approaches to EIS development, but remember to view them strictly from the vantage point of your organizational profile.

Small Is Beautiful

Under this paradigm, small is great, and big is obscene; and the primary difference between the two types of system lies in the profit pocketed by deceptive vendors. The small EIS can do virtually everything a big one can, and often do it better. The small EIS lends itself to flexibility, responsiveness and low cost. Finally, these advocates argue that you are always better off applying your savings to people rather than software. After all, in the final analysis it is people who make the difference.

The issue of EIS size cannot be adequately considered without giving at least equal consideration to what you want to accomplish, your functional requirements. Many of the "small" solutions look very similar to the big, more expensive alternatives because they are viewed in the implicit belief that EIS is electronic reports and charts. Because virtually all systems can deliver information in an easy-to-access fashion, they appear quite similar. If your profile calls for little more than static reporting of information, then look no further. The small EIS is the appropriate solution for you.

Remember that many of these systems offer little or no assistance in data acquisition. They may make no provision for the migration of information, and may not allow for EIS-to-EIS connectivity. Often there is no administrative capability, so every EIS becomes a new EIS. This situation can impede customization.

Despite its limitations, the small EIS can make tremendous sense when your vision is less the optimization of the executive and more the consistent delivery of information. Some organizations, for example, want to create a sales reporting system. Their desire is not to target the executive directly (although he or she may be a user); they prefer to transfer knowledge from the hands of the few into the minds of the many. Because the data is fairly standardized, the number of users can be quite high (cost per user), and no information migration is anticipated. The small EIS may be just the way to go.

Start Small

This is the banner of the risk-averse. The full slogan might be "Start small, fail small." It has been the rallying cry for systems development for decades. Unlike the "small is beautiful" philosophy, the intent here is not to stay with the small technology, but rather to use its success as a springboard.

The "start small" is often called a pilot project by developers. The rationale is that cost should be commensurate with risk—the higher the risk of a project, the lower the cost should be. That way, failure is less damaging. Once its success has been proved, the project risk is lessened, and funding can be increased in recognition of the lower risk.

If one were to look at the back of the "Start small, fail small" banner, one would read "Start small, succeed small." A project that is limited in scope and functionality cannot hope to yield a big win. In fact, proponents of this development approach do not expect a home run. They will declare their intention to move to a more robust, real-world solution once the project's credibility has been established.

There are several major flaws in the pilot approach to development. Foremost from an evaluation perspective, success cannot be leveraged into any meaningful understanding of technological requirements. We are, after all, applying technology that we know is insufficient to our needs. Success only means that those needs were not representative of our profile.

"So what?" exclaimed a pilot proponent. "Who can argue with success? You can always grow the system from there!" But what are the consequences of success? Some organizations find that their executives start migrating in the direction anticipated by the profile, but each *incremental* demand is insufficient to justify the required technology. They become victims of their own success. Many information centers discovered this trap in the 1980s. They delivered success, but were unable to fund the natural migration for the amount and complexity of support required.

What about the growth logic? Could we start with a limited application, and then grow it to more strategic applications of the technology? Theoretically, yes, but in practice this often does not occur. We often do not add more strategic applications, nor do we increase the executive's ability to migrate the information (increase insight). What we do is confuse increased detail with growth.

Now that we have talked about the consequences of success, what of failure? If a pilot fails, what does that tell us? It may not be that we were "not ready for EIS," as I have heard so many people say. After all, we *knew* that the real solution needed to be more vigorous than our pilot. Failure may, in fact, merely confirm what we suspected all along—that for our specific organization, minimum functionality was not enough.

If the pilot approach does not help us in evaluating technology, and is a poor predictor of an organization's readiness for an EIS, why launch a pilot project? Some will argue that pilots can help us garner support, even cultivate a sponsor. It is true that some executives intuitively appreciate the value of the EIS, recognizing how that value will apply to them. More often, however, approval can be merely a vote for sexy technology, dissociated from application benefits. This scenario is often doomed to a cycle of short term success and long term failure.

I am always amazed to hear a member of an EIS project team bemoan the shortsightedness and lack of insight of executives who turn thumbs down on a pilot. "They just don't understand" is the often-heard refrain. Perhaps they understand all too well. The pilot showed the executives minimal functionality, yet was the basis upon which "big EIS" funds were requested. Rather than challenging their wisdom, perhaps we should congratulate them on their perceptivity.

Meat, Potatoes, and an Appetizer

Increasingly, organizations are discovering that the first EIS application must be functional. It must add value, not just display technology. One popular approach is to deliver the monthly briefing book electronically. This usually can be accomplished with a minimum of effort and time, yet it adds value by improving the productivity of the executive.

Unfortunately, the briefing book is unexciting. Most of the information has been delivered to the executive for years. It is useful and can be implemented quickly, but often it lacks the punch needed to engender enthusiastic support. From an evaluation perspective, the application is relatively trivial for most technologies. Unless this is the extent of your vision, briefing-book success will not minimize surprise.

If we consider the briefing book a "meat and potatoes" application, then what we are missing is the appetizer. We need something that will both excite the executive user and stretch the application's value in the evaluation. To ensure that the first application has punch, we need to augment the standard fare with something that will both offer significant added value and contribute to the executive's vision of what the system can become.

How do we select the right appetizer? Ideally, it should have the following characteristics:

- Can be quickly implemented, usually within the first development timetable.

- Is derived from the executive interview.

- Is challenging to the technology.

• Is representative of the ongoing value of the EIS.

Often the best appetizer is some tactical or strategic information that the executive does not currently receive. Almost anything of this nature is significant added value, even if it is significantly incomplete. Most important, this information must reflect the EIS vision. If its practical value to the executive and the organization is not intuitively obvious, save it for another time.

For some excellent ideas on the kind of information that might make look at a good appetizer, see page 491 of Tom Peters's book *Thriving on Chaos.*[1] His sample of unconventional measures represents a small sampling of the kind of information that might make for a good appetizer. Some of his measures are:

• The ten attributes of customer satisfaction.

• The number of small starts.

• The number of ideas "swiped" from competitors per month.

• Hours/dollars devoted to skill upgrading.

• The number of demeaning and debilitating regulations renounced per month.

The Peters measures should be used to provoke ideas, not to limit your thinking. Look to your own organization and the results of your interviews for the ideas with greatest potential.

COMPLEMENTARY AND SUPPLEMENTARY TECHNOLOGIES

Another important decision that must be made concerns what complementary and supplementary technologies are available and functional for your purpose. To the degree that you have access to such technology, this decision can significantly impact the yardstick by which you will judge competing solutions.

Many organizations, for example, have used Harvard Graphics extensively for some time. Any technology that can integrate Harvard Graphics limits its own need for a proprietary graphics capability. Further, as you would expect from an open architecture, such use leverages your existing inventory of graphics output. As long as you think that Harvard Graphics satisfies your functional needs, you can dismiss an EIS product's graphic weakness. For your specific circumstances, that may even be considered a plus.

Continuing with our Harvard Graphics example, I wish to sound a strong note of caution. We can only forgive what would otherwise be a serious weakness *if* the delivered result is functionally unchanged. Perhaps the graphics are difficult or cumbersome to integrate into the delivered result. Maintenance may be an issue, or perhaps integrity degrades for lack of connectivity to the data. Because the graphics are display-only (cannot be manipulated or evolved), they may only be useful as a complement to the EIS software's own picture-making capability. Chart capabilities may still need to evaluated on a stand-alone basis.

Another example of complementary/supplementary technology is in the area of data acquisition. Most organizations have already established some level of competency in this area. As long as it meets the *delivered functionality* test, your evaluation should fully consider this capability.

Naturally, the more diverse the data sources are, the more challenging the acquisition function is. Two inexpensive products are available that belong in virtually every toolkit. In both cases we are not dealing with exclusive products; others also are available. The two mentioned here are viable examples of currently available capabilities.

One of these complementary products is Magic Mirror, from SoftLogic. This is a TSR (terminate, stay resident) utility available for under $100. As long as data can be viewed from your PC (from *any* source), you can highlight and capture that data, transporting it to any other program. Because it is extremely easy to use, and highlighted patterns can be memorized, regular capturing and sharing of data can be a trivial, clerical function. Its value extends beyond sharing between applications, as it is useful for sharing across all hardware and software platforms.

Although products such as Magic Mirror offer an easy solution of high integrity, they are not perfect. Because the interface is manual, these products should be considered functional for relatively low volumes of data. Even if you could automate the selection and capture routines, these solutions could not be considered high-volume tools.

Another excellent product is OmniPage, from Caere. This is an OCR (optical character recognition) product that allows you not only to capture text and numbers as images, but to translate those images into actual numbers and text, as if they were entered by using a keyboard. It is now possible to take information from *any* typed source (including draft mode) and integrate it into the EIS. OmniPage requires a scanner (for roughly $1,000), and costs under $1,000 for the Macintosh or a 386 IBM compatible system. Virtually anything an executive now receives (or might want to receive) can be captured, enhanced, and delivered.

Again, Magic Mirror and OmniPage are not the only products of their type, nor are these the only two categories of complementary technologies. It is incumbent on every EIS team not only to evaluate the formal "EIS offerings", but to understand the availability and limitations of other complementary and supplementary solutions.

When you are considering either complementary or supplementary technologies, it is good practice to ask the vendor to play devil's advocate. Because you are vested in leveraging your existing capabilities, you may not be able to clearly see fundamental weaknesses in your own ideas. Request that a vendor who offers that technology critique your approach. If the vendor cannot provide specific examples of how it will not work for your situation, treat it as a viable complementary or supplementary solution. Remember that such observations cannot be made in the absence of specific details of your EIS. Unless the vendor understands your vision and functional profile, the devil's-advocate approach will not work.

THE SELECTION COMMITTEE

The selection committee is a group of usually part-time evaluators charged with the responsibility of selecting the "appropriate" EIS software. There are several valid reasons for establishing such a committee:

- *CYP (cover your posterior)*—It once was observed that "Sex is only important in a marriage when it's missing." Similarly, good performance in selecting the software rarely brings notoriety to the evaluator. A poor selection, however, can bring swift and deadly visibility to many well-intentioned individuals. Given the impact that software selection can have on corporate resources, most employees desire to share their accountability with others.

- *Group wisdom*—There is a widespread belief in corporations that when it comes to decision-making, many are better than few. Whether minimizing risk or maximizing wisdom, the committee process is often standard operating procedure.

- *Diverse backgrounds*—The past two decades have seen the steady erosion of the melting pot theory. Just as a diversity of backgrounds can enrich our culture, so can it enrich cross-functional decision-making. Because most EIS software will be used by groups from different functional backgrounds, many companies will seek to reflect this mix in the makeup of the committee itself.

- *Carry the ball*—Evaluating EIS software is rarely a full-time activity. Vacations, leaves of absence, closing the books, and special projects are just a few of the many "distractions" experienced by individual evaluators. Safety in numbers means that if one person "drops the flag," there is always another to carry the responsibility.

DEVELOP THE CRITERIA CHECKLIST

There is something deeply satisfying about the creation of a checklist. After all, the selection process is often viewed as a time to bring order to a heretofore disorderly condition. It is precisely in the premise of bringing "order out of chaos," "decisions out of confusion," that most checklists fail.

The usual checklist is created as follows:

1. Poll the users about features required.

2. Ask each user to weight each listed feature on its importance to him or her—usually by required, nice, and not known.

3. List all packages across the top, and check off each feature claimed by each vendor.

4. Based on the assigned priorities, sum up the feature performance of each package.

The problem with this approach is that the evaluators rarely, if ever, are in a position to pick the superior package. On every application, each user comes with an associated group of "high priority" needs that no one package can hope to satisfy. In its most fundamental form, the conflict between priorities becomes: "We would like a product with many features from which to choose. Unfortunately, those with the most features are all older, more mature products. Most of these are not based on the state-of-the-art human factors we require for ease-of-use." Obviously, the more generic the motivation is, the more difficult this tradeoff. How do we evaluate a system's ability to support a range of decisions, most of which have yet to be identified?

Checklist Limitations

The checklist is not a mechanism to resolve differences; it just airs them. Where basic similarities between products exist, this might be sufficient. If products differ in their fundamental architecture and orientation, such an analysis can be totally misleading. Because of its end-user orientation, an EIS package never can be confined merely to a list of existing features.

Many corporate committees have attempted to capture the elusive ease-of-use factor by including it as a feature of a checklist. This might work if usage could be measured without regard to the features being used. A chef cannot evaluate a dish merely according to the taste of the individual ingredients. Only by considering how all the components relate can one be sure of a palatable dish. Evaluating software according to individual features likewise cannot guarantee a "palatable" product.

Most evaluators would be hard pressed to make a confident selection based only on a checklist. No matter how encompassing, few lists leave the evaluators with less than three products at the end of the process. The problem is a basic one. The checklist process usually results in too many checks and too few differences.

As the committee ponders the traditional pages of features on the checklist, remember that few, if any, selections are actually made on that basis.

It is important to maintain a sense of the primary buying motivation, and those features required to ensure success. But even here, the choices may not be simple.

In trying to weigh tradeoffs, keep in mind that the solution may not lie in deciding between one package and another. One corporation had a basic need for a large number of financial functions, as well as a request that all EIS results be communicated to management through the use of high-quality graphics. This created quite a problem, as no package that was evaluated offered both financial functionality and presentation graphics. It was only after exhausting all options that they realized they did not need to satisfy both needs with the same package.They already owned a powerful graphics package, which was quite satisfactory to executive management. Thus they needed a financial package with good software interfacing capabilities. Their software needs were soon satisfied.

I am convinced that in most cases checklist evaluations are not necessary, and in fact can unjustifiably extend the evaluation itself. When they are used, they should be employed as a last resort, left to the end of the evaluation. Doing this will signify that there are two products, both of which will do the job for you. The checklist becomes a tie-breaker.

If in doubt about a particular feature, ask yourself the following question: If this feature were missing, what would be the real business consequences? If you are not sure, the chances are that the feature is not necessary.

WORKING WITH VENDORS

Very little has ever been written on the fine art of working with a vendor during the evaluation. Talk to ten people on this topic, and you are bound to get ten totally different answers, ranging from "It's like a prolonged root canal" to "Very helpful and informative." Many consider this part of the evaluation a necessary evil, which must be endured. This is unfortunate. Many vendors and their salespeople (yes, salespeople) have considerable technology and application knowledge. They also potentially have been through enough evaluations to help you to maximize the benefits while minimizing the pain.

The key word when discussing the vendor's contribution is *potential*. Salespeople do not all equally have something original to contribute, and no vendor can be completely objective. In fact, do not expect this. Vendors and their salespeople are trained and experienced in *their* paradigms. Most (but not all) do not intentionally misrepresent, but they do enthusiastically represent their version of the right solution. The trick is to be a partner with the vendor, letting the vendor understand as much as possible about your vision and profile—but make sure that you control the partnership.

REQUEST FOR PROPOSALS

A request for proposal (RFP) is a way of gathering specific information on the vendor's technology prior to any significant face-to-face interaction. The greater the number of competitive options, the more valuable the RFP becomes. You should not embark on it lightly, however. Proper preparation of the RFP requires considerable effort.

If you decide on an RFP, use your profile to assist in its creation. This will help you to keep down its size, while making sure it fits your needs. The RFP should be preceded by either an oral or a written description of your profile, and you should instruct the vendors only to respond to the functional requirements reflected in that profile. This is very important. Most vendors have their own EIS vision, one that matches the technologies they offer. Insisting that they strictly adhere to *your* profile will avoid uneccesary discussion concerning which vision is right.

If you have strict financial resource limits, make them explicit. Several vendors now have different versions of their products, or alternative packaging to meet a sliding price scale. To be sure you are comparing "apples to apples," they need to understand any price sensitivity.

Design the RFP as the critical minimum that you need to know. Asking fewer questions increases the likelihood that the vendor will put enough thought into each one. I have seen ten-page, 200-question RFPs given to EIS vendors. They cannot possibly put much thought into each question. These large surveys only succeed in extending the evaluation period, because of their response time and your analysis time. You should not consider the RFP as an occasion for gathering *all* the technical information concerning the technology. Its primary function should be to highlight a product's relative fit to your needs.

It is unusual for the RFP stage to result in the selection of more than four viable products. When this occurs, it is usually the result of an RFP that poorly matches the requesting organization's profile. Make every effort to narrow the product choices down to three or four. Any more than this can be unwieldly.

If you have identified any particular problems upon reviewing the RFPs, it might be wise to tell the respective vendors about them. If you do plan not to invite the vendors to present to you on that basis, suggest that they respond quickly, or they will be disqualified. If you plan to invite them despite the issues, insist that they come prepared to discuss those matters.

VENDOR PRESENTATIONS

This is your opportunity to see the product firsthand. It is also the time to learn about the vendor's background, philosophy and plans for the future. Uncontrolled, it is a chance to waste a perfectly good afternoon. To avoid major disappointment, consider the following suggestions:

- Give each vendor a strict time limit for their session. You have a right to do this. Two or three hours should be more than enough time for a vendor to cover all important ground. Make sure the vendors understand that this is all the time they will receive.

- Invite as many directly involved people to the session as possible. This can be trickly, as many more may be interested in EIS. The danger with inviting noninvolved people is that they will not understand the thinking that went into the vision and profile. This can really cause the session to go astray.

- Take care when inviting executives. They also will not appreciate the profile, and may be overly impressed with a slick interface. In one particular set of presentations, one vendor took the time to develop some industry-specific screens, but the other did not. The executive assumed that the one he identified with most was the better one, and the team had a very hard time convincing him otherwise.

  If you do invite executives, divide the session into two parts: the first, high-level part for the executives, the second, more technical part for the other people.

- Consider "suggesting" to the vendor rough approximations of how much time you want to spend on each segment. This way a minimum part of the session will be on nonessential material. Explain in detail exactly what you want covered. At a minimum, vendors should come prepared to discuss unresolved issues, their company's history and stability, the size and nature of the user base, product architecture and technical specifics, and future plans.

- Insist that vendors limit their remarks specifically to your profile. If they start to stray from that path, stop them. Most vendors have boilerplate presentations designed for a one-size-fits-all world. This is wasteful not only of your time, but of theirs as well. This session may not require a customized product demonstration, but does require a customized presentation. Explain that they need not make new slides, but they should exclude those that are not relevant. Further, they should be able to discuss the relevent issues around the slides that already exist.

- Insist that each vendor come prepared with a specific configuration and related price information. This is important. Too many times I have seen a vendor present a solution that seemed to match the host organization's needs perfectly, only to quote the price as "between $40,000 and $200,000, depending on your needs."

The purpose of this first round (yes, first round) of presentations is to allow your team to get a consistent message concerning the various options. It will provide different information from the RFP (if used), and will highlight significant differences between the alternatives. Occasionally an evaluation at this point yields one clear winner. More often you will be facing two; or more rarely, a maximum of three.

With the field narrowed down, the next (vendor screening) phase consists of three distinct parts. (The parts can be pursued simultaneously, and that should be considered if time is an issue.) The three parts are using references, vendor visits, and technology trials.

USING REFERENCES

Most organizations greatly underutilize references. I know of no formal studies on the topic, but my experience suggests that this situation existed six years ago with decision support systems (DSS) and has not improved much since then.

Maybe the problem we have with using references has something to do with the source. We reason that only the most self-destructive vendors will provide the names of organizations that are openly critical of their products. This reminds us of the phrase "References available upon request" found at the end of a résumé. We assume that the reference will supply glowing commentary on the prospective employee, so why bother to check it out?

References in fact offer a wealth of information on the prospective product's strengths and weaknesses. We need only ask the right questions. In fact, I have found that a reference's willingness to spend time on the topic is directly related to the questions asked. The more stretching the questions, the greater the likelihood that the person will open up.

The most important factor in using references is to try to select those that are functionally relevant. Right off the bat, we seem to mess this up! Too many organizations consider industry similarity as a primary criterion, but virtually ignore enormous differences in how the technology is employed. It is not that industry relevance is unimportant. Such contacts can provide valuable *application* information that is useful in EIS development, but application knowledge will not assist us in the evaluation process. Only the proper use of functionally relevant references will do that.

Selecting the Functionally Relevant Reference

The proper use of references is a time-consuming activity. Every effort should be made to thin the ranks of prospective products prior to moving to the reference stage. This should not be a problem if you have a well-thought out profile, and understand how that profile is linked to the technology.

No reference will be able to tell you the right product for your specific needs—there are just too many variables. If you expect to minimize surprise in this way, you undoubtedly will be in for a double surprise. You might be able to fill in some knowledge gaps, but even this may be stretching hope a bit too far. What you can expect from references is a confirmation or a rebuttal of the understanding you gained during the evaluation process. This is especially true when you have doubts about a product's ability to fit within your environment.

The first step is to share with the vendor(s) your EIS profile. Otherwise they cannot help you to identify a fit. Perhaps that is why so many references are only industry-relevant. Even when members of the evaluating organization have established their profile, they keep it secret, afraid to let the vendor too close to their heart. To borrow a term from the government, you can *sanitize* the profile if necessary, but share it as much as possible.

Naturally, no reference will be a perfect fit. If fact, you are almost always far better off assuming no fit, and working to establish compatibility from there. Once the level of compatibility is determined, you need to apply this knowledge to all aspects of the reference interview.

The application of the degree of fit is extremely important, but it can be tricky. I had a client organization whose people did a very thorough job of qualifying the reference. They understood that the vendor's reference was not resource-compatible, being quite constrained by a limited mainframe resource. They avoided the discussion of resources completely, focusing instead on ease of implementation and maintenance.

The reference regaled my client's people with tales so lurid, so ghastly, that they began to doubt the wisdom of even continuing EIS as a project. Among other things, they were told that only the most technically proficient systems professional could even begin to make the software work. They were informed that development took over eight months, and that there were still problems. Executive satisfaction was low, and the demand for future EIS projects had dried up.

On further inspection, they determined that the severe technical problems were largely reflections of the resource issue. Because of such constraints, the reference organization had to use the software in unsupported and nonrecommended ways. Their nightmare, in fact, was a direct result of their own poor performance in conducting an evaluation in a prior year.

One of the central themes of this book is that an adequate understanding of technology should enable you to anticipate not just technology-related problems, but issues relating to both support and delivered functionality. What happened to my client is an excellent example of this interrelationship. With this understanding, the evaluators were able still to make excellent use of the reference. Properly interpreted, almost any reference can provide valuable insight into the predicted performance of a technology.

There is one final consideration before we move on to the reference questions—the challenge we face in evaluating a moving target, because of the inevitable change in products over time. A reference, for example, may reveal serious problems encountered in the modification of the screen design. By all means, give the vendor a chance to respond to this issue, but expect one of two responses: either an explanation of why that problem does not really relate to you, or the claim that the product has changed since then.

Listen to the explanation. It is possible that the vendor sees relationships that you fail to see. But beware of a "totally new product" claim, which can create an intolerable paradox. You want to work with an experienced reference, one who has been down some of the roads you expect to travel, not someone who may not be using the most up-to-date version of the product for many applications. Thus, it is not unusual for a vendor to argue that the problems that are identified by a mature reference are made irrelevant by a new, improved version of the product. You should listen to the good stuff, and not worry excessively about the bad. Listen to both the good and the bad.

The first set of questions for the reference should be designed to establish fit. Remember that lack of compatibility in a specific area does not discredit the reference, but it does suggest that the evaluator treat with great caution the specific area of nonfit as well as any areas that are logically connected to it. The following should not be considered a complete list of questions. It is up to each evaluating organization to add to and customize the questions as appropriate to their unique circumstances. If the reference has more than eighteen months' experience, most questions should be asked for the first six months as well as for the longer time frame.

- *Number of executives*—There is a big difference between supporting ten and supporting fifty.

- *Frequency and duration of use*—I know of one organization that considers its EIS to be wildly successful; yet its executives use the system fifteen minutes per month. If you believe that is worth the investment, there is no problem with that criterion of success. For many organizations, such use would equate to failure.

- *Literacy of executives*—Some organizations have executives with considerable computer literacy. As a group they may be far more tolerant of a complex interface, and far less tolerant of status-only reporting.

- *Diversity of executives*—We have already spoken of the increased demands a heterogeneous EIS can place on the technology. Success with a sales EIS may not equate to success for the diverse staff of a CEO.

- *Age of system (with growth curve)*—It is important to know not only the age of their EIS, but also its growth over that time. Be particularly sensitive to systems that never seemed to "take off," and systems with high early growth that stalled or dropped. Although there might be perfectly reasonable explanations for growth problems, these responses can highlight issues you are better off knowing.

- *Nature of the EIS*—Is it an issue-based EIS, centering on crisis reporting? A financial reporting system? Appreciating how it is used will help you evaluate the relevancy of its success.

- *Diversity of data sources*—Where does the data come from? Is any third-party technology used to assist in access or preparation?

- *FTE support*—Including the providers, what is the FTE (full time equivalent) headcount? What about excluding the providers? How many technical support persons are there? With this information you can calculate various support ratios that are valuable in comparing and predicting performance.

- *Hardware configurations*—What is the hardware type and configuration? What about machine loading (percent to capacity)?

After you have established system compatibility, the next step is to help the reference help you to determine the technology's strengths and weaknesses. My suggestion is to start with open-ended questions and get more specific as the discussion progresses (see Figure 12-1). It is important to probe as many aspects of the reference's experience as possible. Quite often a question will trigger the memory of a situation that could be quite relevant to you. You only learn by asking.

The following questions may be particularly useful:

- *Are you happy with your EIS?*—You may as well get the obvious out of the way.

- *Were there any surprises after your evaluation?*—This may spark one of those memories we were talking about. It could also give you some helpful ideas for your current investigation.

- *Were there any surprises during implementation?*—The concept is the same as the above. This is especially important if the reference is at a mature EIS site. Because the system is in the maintenance mode, implementation problems may have been forgotten. This question may help the reference remember.

- *Were there any surprises in maintaining the system?*

- *When did you purchase the product? Have you kept it current?*—Do not laugh. I have seen cases where the reference had selected the product years before, when the only viable competition was a fourth-generation language. Remember, all technology assessments are relative.

- *What do you like about the product? Dislike?*—You may think this question is too obvious, but it often works very well. The question of dislikes is especially important. It causes a psychological reaction—if you ask for negatives following a request for positives, people will stretch to give you some weak points, even if they are not very relevant to them. In this way they do not feel naive. A weak point that is not very important to them may be critical to you.

- *What do you consider the most important advantages of your EIS?*—Most organizations never constructed a vision or profile. The best you can do is to try to back into their EIS vision by asking this question. Does it match your vision?

- *Do you know any organizations that have had problems? Can you provide a contact?*—At least you may identify some important issues. Many organizations network with others with an EIS. This is a way to combine multiple references into one.

- *What is the attitude of the executives concerning the EIS? What do they think the benefits are?*—We are trying to distinguish between the technology's benefits as marketed by the vendors and the *delivered benefits* experienced by the reference.

1. When did you purchase? _____

   _____

2. Why did you decide on this product? _____

   _____

   _____

   _____

3. What other software did you consider? _____

   _____

   _____

   _____

4. What applications are currently in use? _____

   _____

   _____

   _____

5. Is this supported by business professionals? Extent? _____

   _____

   _____

   _____

6. What is the ratio of users vs. support people? Why? _____

   _____

   _____

   _____

7. What are the biggest benefits of your application? _____

   _____

   _____

   _____

[1] Ask for 2-4 references. The same industry is nice but usually not necessary.

Figure 12-1. Reference query form.

8. What has been your biggest support problem?   _____

_____

_____

_____

9. What has been your biggest technical challenge?   _____

_____

_____

_____

10. What is your machine configuration, loading, performance?

_____

_____

_____

11. What do you consider the product's strengths?   _____

_____

_____

_____

12. What do you consider the product's weaknesses?   _____

_____

_____

_____

13. How would you rate the vendor's support? Why?   _____

_____

_____

_____

14. What other companies (contacts) can you recommend?

_____

_____

_____

Figure 12-1. (cont.)

- *What is the attitude of the support staff?*—Look for responses such as "overworked," "no support," "no IS cooperation," or "resisted by business providers."

- *Do you use the business specialists as providers? If not, why not?*—If this is important to you, the answer could provide a danger signal.

- *How do you rate the vendor's support?*—Sometimes the reference will answer in black or white, but often you will get answers such as "Easy to contact them, but I know more than they do," or "Hard to connect, but very knowledgable when you do."

- *What other technologies did you look at? Why?*—This not only helps you to understand their frame of reference, but may suggest a product you overlooked.

- *What made you decide on this product versus a competitor's?*— The answer potentially can give you insight into either the product they are using or perhaps some deficiency in another product you have not identified.

- *What other organization (and contact) do you recommend that we speak to?*—This can be your most important question. Make sure the reference understands something of your profile. By asking this question, you often can circumvent the dilemma of having the vendor suggest only positive references. It is neither illegal nor unethical to use references not certified by the vendor. It can, however, be quite valuable.

Remember to be flexible in your interview. Regard these questions as suggesting a direction for the discussion. This attitude will keep the conversation open, increasing the likelihood of your uncovering the unexpected. Try to use the same active listening skills that you employed during the executive interviews. This should help you even if your discussion is done by telephone.

Can a conversation with a reference be adequately handled over the phone? In most cases, this is no problem. If you can work with a reference on-site, it usually is preferable to do so. Given the time and logistical demands of person-to-person meetings, this effort implies special diligence on your part in qualifying the reference to your situation.

ATTENDING USER GROUP MEETINGS

If your timing is fortunate enough, plan to attend a user group meeting hosted by the vendors. These meetings usually occur annually, and can bring together hundreds of users, depending upon the size of the installed base. Besides affording one an excellent opportunity to make contact with unofficial references, they provide a global view of the product that would otherwise be impossible to achieve.

It is important to keep a level head during these meetings, as you can easily be pulled in either of two extreme directions. At one end are the vendor and your sales representative. They naturally want this experience to be positive and enthusiastic, and will most likely direct you to those individuals and sessions that reflect their attitude.

At the other end are those users who view the meeting as an opportunity to lobby for specific changes. On balance, they may be quite satisfied with their product selection, but they have come with a specific agenda, which often is skewed toward the negative. They may not spend much time addressing the positive aspects of the product—these have already been achieved. Instead they will focus on those things yet to be delivered. This attitude can be perceived as quite negative.

The best you can do is keep in mind this tendency toward extremes. Take notes of everything you see, and collect business cards as if they were gold. Be sure to continue to network. Networking will never be more important than at this time. Do not fall into the trap of locking into your industry comfort zone. If you have not spoken to at least ten new people each day, you are not doing your job.

VENDOR VISITS

Once you have trimmed the field, even if you have selected the product of choice, you should always seriously consider visiting the corporate headquarters of the vendor(s). The visit delivers several important benefits:

- *Strategic perspective*—Often your sales representative does not know all the R&D directions planned by the vendor. Because this effort directly impacts your ability to grow and thrive with your EIS, its understanding is critical.

- *Technical perspective*—Perhaps some technical issues have not been adequately explained to you. Even the best local technical support person will have limits. At the vendor's headquarters you have access to the system developers. The more important the issue, the more valuable it is to hear it from the "horse's mouth."

- *Development perspective*—Frequently the local sales office is not privy to the next release of the product. Even if they know about some of it, they rarely can demonstrate it. A vendor visit provides you the opportunity to get "hands on" with the next release. Be aware, however, that you may have to sign a nondisclosure agreement on what you hear and are shown. If it is required, ask for a copy in advance, so that your legal department can have the opportunity to approve it first.

- *Executive perspective*—This has a dual purpose: you get the opportunity to converse with the vendor's senior executives, and your senior management get the opportunity to discuss EIS at a very high level as well. Although you ideally might like for your executives (or some of them) to visit all vendors, it is more likely that they will visit just one vendor. If you must choose, prioritize the vendors and suggest the most likely one.

The key to the vendor visit is preparation. Treat it as your last opportunity to get the information you need. Consolidate all remaining questions/issues and your objectives, and distribute your list to the appropriate vendor. That way the vendor can prepare for the visit, making sure to best meet your needs. If necessary, divide your evaluation group into segments—one segment listening to the strategic direction, for example, while the other addresses the technical issues.

TECHNOLOGY TRIALS[2]

Following the evaluation path described above, it may not be necessary to have the products battle it out. My experience is that in most cases technology trials consume considerable time. If the evaluation is properly conducted, in fact, the extra effort seems to do nothing more than confirm what most evaluators expected anyway.

Occasionally, however, even the best run evaluation cannot suffice. Sometimes a vocal minority of team members is not convinced of one solution's superiority over another. Or the claims and counterclaims leave you unsure. If this is the case, consider a technology trial.

Depending on how you conduct this part of the evaluation, it can be either be the best or quite often the worst part of the process. The recommendation that follows is not etched in stone. It is a practical and efficient method of comparing technologies, one designed to test the vendor claims, but more important, to highlight differences. I call this approach a shoot-out, as it is quick and produces a clear winner. Armed with that knowledge, you should be able to make up your mind with confidence.

The first step (not surprising) is to pull out your profile. It will guide you in the customizing process that follows. Because your longer-term requirements are usually the most demanding, draw on that part of the profile. Create a scenario that matches as closely as possible the requirements of the profile. Understand that you will not be able to duplicate that profile, but start out with as close an approximation as possible.

Remember that we are trying to test and compare the product's limits. It is uneccesary for the trial application to test the capabilities that you think are already missing or deficient. It is usually not necessary to make the EIS as large as you expect it to become, because increased size rarely equates to corresponding limits. If you think that size may become an issue, then build the system by using generated values and reports. Just do not let the construction details become the project.

As you begin to plan the trial application, try this approach: At the top of a sheet of paper, write three column heads—"Profile," "Capabilities," "Impact." You fill in the columns as follows:

- *Profile*—In this column you will list the functional requirements that you think need to be tested. Again, the key is to prioritize them, on the basis of the areas about which you are most certain. A common mistake here is to list all critical requirements. There is little to gain from covering ground that you have already established. Concentrate on the few areas that you have yet to differentiate or substantiate.

- *Capabilities*—This column will capture those specific technical areas that directly and indirectly relate to the requirements. For example, if an entry under "Profile" is "customized delivery," then the business provider fit-for-use, maintenance, and possibly executive manipulation could be listed here.

  Notice that for one "Profile" item, there can be several listed capabilities. This is not unusual. In fact, it is often because of this hybrid relationship that we have difficulty making clear distinctions between technologies.

- *Impact*—This category deals with those roles that are impacted by the capability. In the above example, you might include the administrator, the executive, and the provider.

The first two columns will help you decide what you want to see. The "Impact" column tells you from what perspective you need to see it. When designing the trial, prepare for it as much as possible beforehand. If you want to use five standard reports, consider providing four of the five to the vendors well in advance of the trial. They can create those without using your time. However, consider asking them to create the fifth report on the spot.

Often, although size may not be an issue in planning the trial application, complexity is critical because it directly impacts maintainability and administration. The point is not to create an application more complex than you expect to tackle. Most organizations err in the other direction. They mistakingly assume that size is the best test of performance under fire—which is rarely the case.

Resource efficiency is the one notable exception to the complexity versus size issue. Here we often need to test a full complement of capabilities, including ease of use, integrity and resource capabilities as they interrelate. There is no acceptable means of resource testing except to use a volume of data representative of your EIS needs.

When you evaluate resource efficiency, the good news is that it need not require the same ad hoc test that the other trial might, as large-volume data access is rarely unplanned. If you need to test resouce utilization (often not required), the vendor can set up the test days prior to the trial. You need only specify the data sources and the desired end result.

Although it is important to help the vendor to prepare, it is critical that you not give the vendor the entire picture. The vendor may protest, but remember that when using the product, you will be largely learning the design of the system as you go. The best laid plans can and do go astray. Let the vendor prepare the pieces you think you can prepare for, but not see the gestalt.

Try to design the trial so that it takes no more than four hours. Prioritize the tasks so that running out of time becomes an inconvenience, not a disaster. Strongly suggest that the vendor sends the best possible person to do the computer work. I have seen a vendor perform poorly and then (after the fact) blame an inexperienced person with whom the host organization worked. Also, it is a good idea to schedule the trial in the afternoon. That way, when you are done, you can take the vendor's representative out for a much-needed drink.

What is the value of "Impact"? We have seen that differences in capabilities can disproportionately affect different individuals. The fact that something is easy for the executive does not mean that it will not negatively impact the administrator. If a capability impacts a particular organizational role, you need to see how that role needs to respond.

Some of my clients initially object to the shoot-out because they are not actually doing the work. They are concerned that this is not an adequate test of ease of use. Under the best of circumstances, they may be right, but rarely do we work under the best of circumstances. What are the alternatives?

- All team members get trained on the final products. This is very wasteful. Because you will select only one product, you will be spending considerable time on at least one product you will never use.

- Divide the team in half, each covering a different product. This is twice as good as the prior solution because you waste only half as much time. Everyone will look at products differently, however; so how can you make a good comparison? Besides, half of your time is still a great deal of time to waste.

The ultimate dilemma in using a hands-on approach is that you can never hope to become proficient in the amount of time you will have. As a matter of fact, the most you can hope to become is dangerous! If you have problems, you will always wonder whether to blame yourself, or your lack of experience with the technology. If you use the vendor's best person, this cloud is removed.

Last, but perhaps most important, always evaluate the EIS techology *as it will be used,* not built. Too often we evaluate a technology from a builder's perspective. We create some screens, establish communications, bring in data, and see how the system performs. Although this is a valid perspective, it rarely will reflect the executive's mode of operation. That is, we implicitly assume that if the system can be built and "works," then the evaluation is complete.

The question of how well the system works can be considered in this way only if static access of screens of information matches your expectation of how the executives will use the EIS. If, however, your vision takes them beyond static delivery of reports and charts, then the technology must be considered in a more dynamic mode. Try exploring some issues (real or fictitious), or perhaps communicating the results of that exploration to another executive. If you evaluate the system as it will be used, you will truly understand the strengths of the technology. If you expect your executives to become explorative, then test for exploration. Testing for system building is okay, but to minimize surprise, use the system.

One approach for testing "fitness for use" is to draft a scenario of six month's usage. Include both *what* an executive may want to do and *how* she or he may want to do it. Then reduce the scenario to its critical mass (eliminating repetitive activities) and use that as a screen for appropriate technology.

REFERENCES

1.   *Thriving on Chaos: Handbook for a Management Revolution,* Tom Peters, Alfred A. Knopf, New York, 1987, pp. 491–492.

2.   I have deliberately used the term "technology trial" rather than "benchmark test." Within the ranks of information systems, the benchmark is commonly held to be a series of tests concerning the technical performance of the product, which is most often conducted *independent of the application*. What typically gets tested is performance, not necessarily performance during use.

The introduction of the "technology trial" is not intended to confuse, but rather to underscore the critical performance of testing for use rather than testing for machine performance. I apologize if this has caused any confusion.

13

Building Your EIS

Some designs become standards because of their timeless functionality. Form contributes to function in a powerful and compelling way. These designs are emulated and enhanced over time. Nature's thousands of designs give ample testimony to this truth.

Other designs become standards because they have the power of precedence. Their only true contribution is that they were first. Every enhancement, every permutation of that standard gives testimony not to its correctness, but its existence. The bicycle seat is an example of this effect. Called a saddle, it reflects the same basic design first established as a saddle for a horse.

Notice that the way we ride a bicycle is quite different from the way we ride a horse. The result can be an irritating experience. Notice also that there are alternatives, such as the split seat (Easy Seat). Although the latter is more comfortable and energizing than the saddle, most of us continue using the old design—not because it is better, but because it was first.

EIS design has fallen into the same trap. The purpose of this chapter is to provide some new perspectives on the design and implementation of executive information systems. It is not suggested that you necessarily use all design options at once. You may want to consider having your system migrate in some of the suggested directions. Even if you never use any of the suggestions, they may motivate your search for designs offering an alternative to the sea of sameness that now exists.

PLANNING YOUR IMPLEMENTATION

When EIS was in its infancy (some would argue that it still is), we all needed to sell the idea, to be cheerleaders for this emerging technology. This, unfortunately, led to oversell; the technology was the victim of too much hype. When these systems invariably failed to live up to the great expectations, they were often perceived as failures. The problem was less what they did than what they did not, or could not do.

Controlling Growth

The common wisdom became "manage expectations." We discovered that an inability to deliver on promised benefits (real or implied) was just as damaging as any other deficiency. This lesson is still an important one. But as most of us have learned to curb our natural enthusiasm in promoting EIS benefits, we have been less than successful in curbing growth.

It may seem strange to spend a vast amount of time trying to garner support and create demand, only to pull back before the first system is delivered. Yet uncontrolled growth is a very real cause of EIS failure, and the time to control that growth is before, not after, implementation begins.

The good news is that planning growth should not take much time or effort. All the pieces are already in place. Armed with our profile, support projections and selected technology, we should have a reasonable idea of the number and the nature of executive information systems we can support over time. This should be the limit of our commitment.

It is not unusual for an organization to discover incredible pent-up demand for EIS once it begins to be unveiled. This can be a very dangerous time. It is up to the implementation team members to hold to their plan and not release more systems than they can comfortably support. You must ignore (or manage) those executives who will say, "All I want is these basic reports, and then I'll be happy." The half life of such requests is no more than six months. After that, either they stop using their systems ("It wasn't that good"), or they will come back to you. It will not matter whether you are ready to support them.

The best way to manage the demand for EIS is to allow your implementation plans to get visibility. Allow all executives to see where their names are as part of the planned rollout. This will not guarantee patience, but it will help. Another approach is to introduce EIS on a division-by-division basis, rather than throughout the corporation. This does not always work. One of my clients tried it, but divisional cross-talk was common. Soon most of the divisions were clamoring for an EIS, far outstripping her ability to support them. The best tool in your arsenal is the word "no."

Content and Justified Expense

If your best weapon is to say no, than your second best is content-justified expense. This concept extends beyond support. It involves the very heart of EIS itself.

Every time our family visited my mother-in-law, she would tell us the same rueful story about remodeling. She and her sister were having their kitchens redone by the same carpenter at the same time. During remodeling, she asked how much more it would cost to extend the cabinets to the ceiling. "That would be prohibitively expensive," was the reply. She decided against it.

Her sister, coincidentally, asked the same question of the carpenter. He again said it would be "prohibitive." "How prohibitive are we talking about?" she asked. "Four hundred dollars," he responded. My mother-in-law always regretted not asking that simple question, especially when visiting her sister's extra spacious kitchen.

Content-justified expense means that you should avoid the presumption that the delivery of certain information, or the support of a certain number of systems, would be "prohibitively" expensive. I constantly see examples where implementation teams cheat themselves and their organizations by presuming an acceptable level of support. This level is always arrived at *independently* of the benefit being delivered. It never hurts to ask if management is willing to support a particular level of delivery.

One approach is to create two or even three implementation plans, each reflecting a different level of total functionality. For each plan, include both the benefits and the related costs (time, headcount, and money). If you find that the demand for growth begins to outstrip your ability to support the EIS, pull out the next plan, and *ask for management commitment*. Do not make the mistake of assuming the costs are "prohibitive." You may be surprised.

NAVIGATION RULES

Navigation provides the user with the ability to find his or her way within the EIS design. The dilemma we frequently face is that simple navigation is often easy, but cumbersome and limiting. Sophisticated navigation can be quite complex and frustrating, but can enhance effectiveness and efficiency. The discussion of navigation explores these relationships and offers some ideas that might free you from this trap.

Menus and Levels

The story is told of a poet who, when writing to a friend, said, "I must apologize for the length of this letter. I didn't have the time to make it brief." That captures the problem we have in designing the EIS navigation. When we plan menus, it is much easier to create more rather than less.

Think of the way we normally regard menus. We present a set of options, asking the users what they want to see or do next. They make selections, and, on the basis of those selections, may see another set of options. The more they potentially can see, the more menus they must navigate. The approach is simple and straightforward, but is heavily oriented toward the developer's sense of easy navigation, not the user's.

All users are interested in information, not menus. The menu is merely a means to an end. Anything that separates users from their objective is a nuisance at best, a frustration at worst. That is the central problem: the developer sees the menu as a means to an end, but the user sees it as a nuisance.

Look at the top of Figure 13-1. The user needs to move down four different menus before seeing any information on European pricing of Gadgets. If this were broken down further, perhaps by country and packaging, six or more menus would be required *before* the user saw any information at all!

As a general rule, try to keep the maximum number of menus navigated before information (critical menus) to three. This is not easy. You may, in fact, find it too daunting a target at first. Accept it as a goal, and see how close you can come. Without that mental stretch, most designers revert back to the six-plus menu approach. Here are some suggestions to help you minimize your critical menus:

- *Matrix menus*—Building a matrix will at a minimum condense two menus into one. The bottom of Figure 13-1 shows that the user can avoid the region menu by combining it with the product menu.

- *Scrolling and pop-up menus*—If the technology will support it, proper use of scrolling and pop-up options can make an incredible difference in reducing critical menus. Figure 13-2 is such a menu. It begins by offering the user four categories: Personnel,

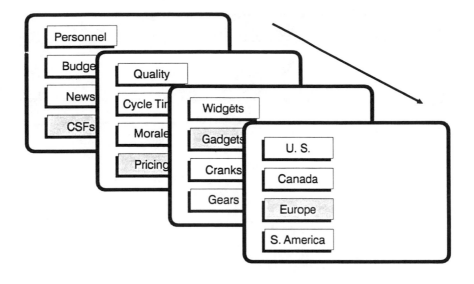

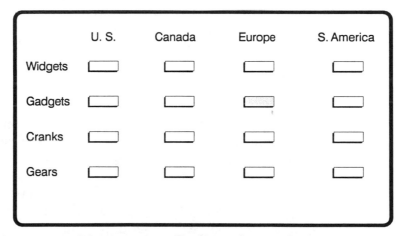

Figure 13-1. Matrix menus. Traditional menu design creates a waterfall effect—one level of options leading to another. Matrix menus can simplify the interface and reduce the number of critical menus that the executive user must navigate.

Budgets, CSFs, and News. If one selects CSFs, the top bar appears, listing four critical success factors: Quality, Cycle Time, Morale, and Pricing.

If the response time is good, the user will feel as if he or she is merely entering the proper settings. If it does not *feel* like menus, it does not frustrate like menus.

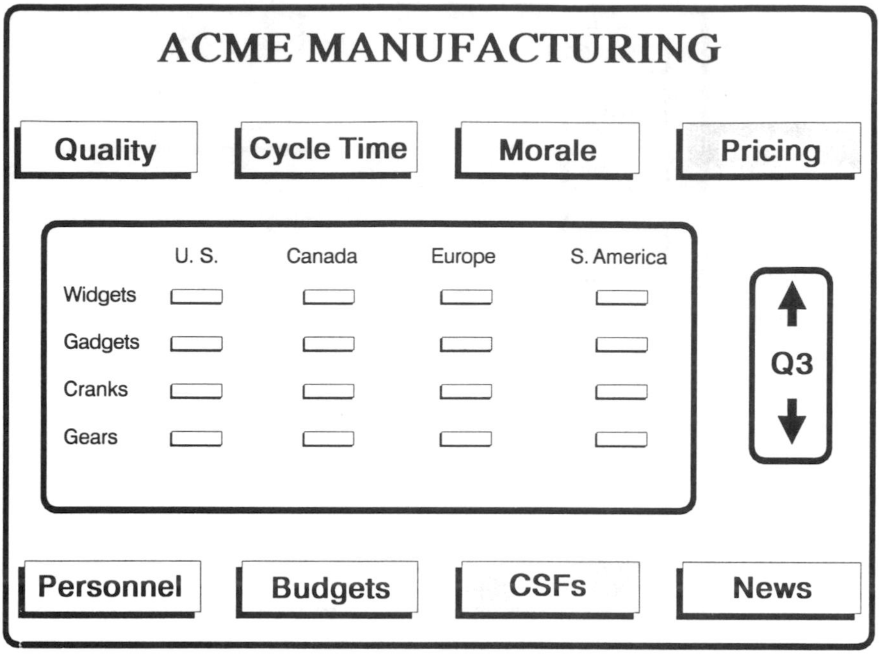

Figure 13-2. Pop-up and scrolling menus. Careful use of pop-up and scrolling menus can present a control panel to the executive, combining a sophisticated set of options into one simple screen.

Continuing with Figure 13-2, if the Pricing CSF is selected, the middle window appears (pop-up), and we see the familiar matrix menu. Notice that on the right we have a new option, setting the proper time period. A user can now scroll up or down (using the arrows) to select the desired quarter.

The menu in Figure 13-2 combines all four original menus, plus the time period menu, on one screen. This is not always easy, but it can be done.

- *Dated menus*—In Figures 13-1 and 13-2, the menus contained options but no information. Think of the frustration of the executive user navigating through four or more menus, just to discover that he or she has already seen the information. Why should the user play a guessing game?

  Figure 13-3 is an example of a dated menu. By placing the date on the option button, the user can instantly see what is old information. If you help the user avoid unnecessary navigation of menus, you essentially reduce the critical menus to zero.

- *Color-coded menus*—Often the executive user is not just looking

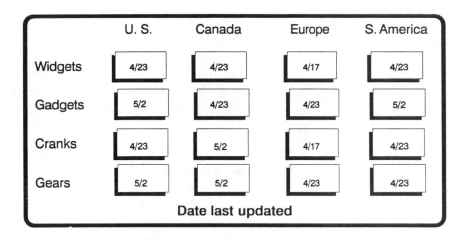

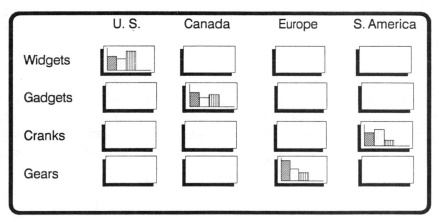

Figure 13-3. Dated and Information Menus. The use of dated and information menus can eliminate the executive's need to select all the menu options. This is perhaps the ultimate in critical menu design.

for information, but is hoping to quickly identify a problem. The concept of color-coding exceptions is an attempt to do just that. By coloring the menu buttons green (performance above expectation), yellow (within expectation), or red (below expectation), the user can avoid selecting options that are not of immediate interest. This is especially valuable for persons who manage by exception.

- *Information menus*—As helpful as color coding is, it unfortunately represents a rather imprecise way of scanning performance. After all, how bad was the red performance? True, you could use different shades of colors to reflect degree of performance, but this could get very complicated (and confusing).

  The bottom half of Figure 13-3 illustrates the use of information menus. Like color-coding, these menus can dramatically reduce your critical menus. Because they contain a summary graph, however, the user now knows the degree to which performance is out of tolerance.

Naturally, some care is required in designing the menu structure. Some people get carried away with the challenge, assuming that every screen must reduce the critical menus. There may be times when you deliberately wish to use a standard menu design.

Another natural (but abused) limit to menus is the physical screen limit. With the increasingly popular graphical executive information systems comes the opportunity to include an extremely crowded menu design. The fact that a designer *can fit* sixty menu buttons on a screen does not obligate that person to use them all. One of the genuine challenges facing EIS is that of good taste.

Use of Color

If good taste is a problem with menu design, it becomes an even greater challenge when one is working with colors. This challenge is not a new one to organizations. Desktop publishing has given information providers the opportunity to use dozens of fonts and report formats. Some feel obligated to use them all, sometimes in the same report.

Color also can be terribly abused. One of the roles that the EIS implementation team (often the administrator) should assume is the setting of color standards of conduct. The rule of thumb is no more than three colors on a single screen. There are exceptions to this rule, but considering the potential for abuse, the exceptions should be used sparingly.

The purpose of an EIS is to intelligently and intuitively guide the executive to information that is most meaningful at a particular time. Color and design can be powerful tools toward that end when combined with the business knowledge of the information provider. Used as a form of artistic expression, the EIS can distract the executive user from the content, rather than enhance its message.

Make Sure It Works

Sometimes an idea sounds reasonable from a developer's perspective, but misses the mark when viewed by the user. An example of this design flaw is the use of menu buttons to inform one of work-in-process.

Recently I was shown an EIS that had been in use for four months. This organization had formed an EIS development committee, consisting of key information providers and the implementation team. The committee had decided it would be a good idea to create a series of new menu options for the executives. Their selections would inform them of a new area of planned development.

If an executive selected the "Key Competitors" button, a description of what would appear in the future was displayed. In all, eleven new "announcement" buttons were added. The committee's logic was that the executives would be imbued with a spirit of growth and energy. Instead, a game developed of "Guess what's behind door number three?"

The problem with announcement buttons is that they are of interest only the first time that they are selected. They often stay in the EIS for many months, and the executives begin to learn that some of the system does not work. Now they need to remember which are the functional and which the nonfunctional buttons. A new level of frustration has been added.

Announcement buttons need not always be avoided. They can achieve the desired level of anticipation. To succeed they must be used judiciously, with a minimum of lead time. If, for example, a new option will be offered next month, it might be an excellent idea to add a little pre-release hype. But the next month, that information had better appear. Any menu option that announces a new offering should have a maximum life of one month.

Design for Control

We have discussed the objective of no surprise for the EIS evaluators. The same target should be used in designing your system. The user should always feel in control.

How do you enhance control? Make sure that the executive can anticipate the result of every selection. There should never be any question about the action that will follow a menu button's being pressed.

One client had a distributed EIS, part functioning on the microcomputer, the rest operating on the mainframe. The EIS design was intended to maximize transparency (minimize awareness of when the user was on the micro or the mainframe), and succeeded in all but one area—response time. When an executive was operating on the mainframe, the system seemed to slow significantly.

The designers reasoned that the mainframe offered such extra value to the executive that this was not a problem. In fact, they were right. None of the executives minded the delayed response time because they expected a high added-value. Because the design was so transparent, however, sometimes the executives would inadvertently select a mainframe option *without the expectation of added-value*. At their very next opportunity, they would jump back to the micro.

Always design the EIS so that the user can anticipate the results of any action. To do otherwise is to lay landmines throughout the EIS. Remember, an executive rarely gets blown up alone.

CUSTOMIZED VS. STANDARDIZED

We have been discussing many of the challenges associated with EIS construction. With so much potential for problems, some organizations have established strict standardization policies. All providers are given severe limits on their options, which virtually eliminate many of the design issues covered here.

Another advantage of standardization is that it provides a nice, uniform look to the EIS. If minimizing surprise is the goal, this becomes the Holy Grail. Because every menu is alike, there is virtually no chance for surprise.

The downside to standardization is that it is boring. True, it is not the objective of the EIS to excite, but it can offer something in between. It does not have to be a black or white situation.

Another, perhaps more important, reason to allow customization is that it permits for context-sensitive design. This can both enhance the message and allow another level of expression on the part of information providers. The more they can add value to the EIS, the more likely they are to be willing to contribute. Ask them to just "fill in the blanks," and you increase the likelihood they will not see an advantage to their participation.

To some degree the question of standardization is one of corporate culture. Some organizations take a very utilitarian view of EIS, and consider "clever menus" a waste of time and effort. Others consider these creative designs the spice of life, and encourage diversity. There is no single right approach.

You may want to consider initiating your EIS with a mix of standards and degrees of freedom. Allow for some creativity, and see the reaction of the users. If it seems positive, you can always give creativity more room in the future. Being too expressive initially can give the wrong message, before the EIS has had a chance to establish a legitimate business purpose.

HYPERTEXT DESIGN

Hypertext is a technology that allows the designer to cross-reference information by intuitively suggesting those paths the user may wish to explore next. Unlike a book's index, in hypertext the cross-references can be embedded directly into the material. The information content suggests options to the user. Selecting one of those options, the user is immediately presented with the referenced material.

In some ways, drill down is like hypertext. The designer has other information relevant to what the user is seeing. This path is suggested by indicating that the item is "drillable." The user then is immediately presented with the next level of detail supporting that number.

Drill down is a very limited version of hypertext, however, because the direction of the jump (the cross-reference) is always in one direction—down. Although this is certainly useful, it puts extraordinary limits on the potential of the EIS. These limits often are not a function of the technology, but of our concept of how that technology can be applied.

Consider for a moment the executive who is viewing a sales problem. Drill down may help explain *what* is being affected, but not necessarily *why*; so the executive can move up to the main menu, select marketing, and begin to drill down that segment. Finally finding the relevant reports, the executive sees that marketing does not seem to be the problem. Moving back to the main menu, he or she next may explore distribution, to see if the problem lies there.

The approach described above is an extreme. You would expect that the information provider would anticipate the executive's concerns, and might add a commentary to the sales report stating that the drop in revenue was due to delays in distribution. The provider could reference the related distribution information, or even include some of the data there. But an executive who wants to see all of the relevant information has no choice but to go back to the main menu and search for it.

Hypertext design allows the information provider to add value to the commentary by offering a menu pick that can take the user directly to the section(s) of the EIS that relate to the represented issue. This eliminates a great deal of navigation on the part of the executive. In addition, the speed with which relevant information can be viewed enhances browsability, which is very important to the executive style and insight.

What we are describing here is not a hypertext system. This technology certainly may become an integral part of EIS, but most likely will require several years before becoming mainstream. We are proposing the use of the hypertext cross-referencing concept where appropriate. Its lack of popularity today is neither a reflection of limited technology nor of complexity, but rather of our own limited paradigm of how information can be presented. Only we can take responsibility for breaking those limits.

Appendix

Appendix A   Sample Interview Notes

This appendix includes sanitized and modified notes from a series of interviews with one of my clients. Selection of these notes was not based on quality, as much of the best information had to be removed because of its sensitive nature. They were chosen because they are based on a sales EIS. Because sales is often one of the most focused and tactical of functions, it represents a particular challenge to the interviewer.

All the notes were organized by using an outlining software package. If you are not familiar with outlining software, consider it a "must" before beginning any interviews. I use Maxthink (415-540-5508), perhaps the best outlining product, but most popular products will meet your minimum needs.

You will probably want to consider your own variations on my documentation style. This specific design is intended both to inform and to further sell the concept of EIS and its benefits. Remember that the review notes, like every other contact you will have with your executives, provide you an opportunity to cultivate a sponsor. Do not squander this chance by treating the interview notes as a purely technical component of the EIS project.

REPORT ON EXECUTIVE INTERVIEWS: MICHTEK

Executive Summary

MichTek is an excellent candidate for an executive information system. The interviews indicated a very high potential for added-value to executive management.

MichTek is quite fortunate in that information systems has established a good foundation upon which to deliver much of the targeted material, and market research has created an excellent pool of information from which to draw. Because of this, the first-phase EIS should be of significant value, and deliverable in three to five months.

The interview results reflect a sophisticated understanding of MichTek's business environment, as well as an appreciation of emerging challenges. The general philosophy behind the results seems to recognize the need to become more proactive. This can be seen in the expressed desire for early detection, intervention, and monitoring of activities.

We should sound a cautionary note concerning two points. The first is regarding the apparent overemphasis on older lines versus newer lines. While it is true that older lines constitute the majority of *today's* business, it seems generally recognized that much of the future business needs to come from newly added lines. The emphasis of new markets requires superior performance and early interdiction, two things an EIS can enhance.

The second is the historical bias of most information at MichTek. This bias is understandable, given the long and stable history of the older lines. During this extended period of stability, quick response and anticipation were relatively unimportant. Today, they are critical. This is a different approach to information, and one that MichTek has only begun to explore.

Summary of Interview Results

There were four primary capabilities requested during the interviews: productivity, exploration, early warning, and leadership.

Productivity

There is always an advantage in being able to access required material more quickly. Some sales and financial information, for example, is already accessible to the individual executive. Because of its paper form, however, the format might be more of an obstacle than an aid.

When speed and ease of access are at sufficient levels, we can move beyond productivity and actually improve our ability to draw insights from the information. Because we can quickly "browse" important material, we can gain perspectives that otherwise may have escaped us.

Exploration

The limitation of paper reporting is that it must necessarily address the lowest common denominator of perspective. To support every possible way an executive might want to look at the numbers would otherwise require literally thousands of reports. Yet virtually every executive expressed the need to look at sales results in a multitude of ways: account, product, business unit, etc.

Leveraging off the existing IS database, an executive information system (EIS) can provide each executive with the ability to easily manipulate the information. The reports are created without effort, on demand, in a format meaningful to each individual executive.

Early Warning

The problem with strategic challenges is that they rarely show themselves with a frequency that warrants regular viewing. The tactical ones receive daily attention, but the strategic issues may be ignored until they move into the crisis, or tactical arena.

The EIS can serve as an early warning system. Shifting markets, prices, purchasing patterns, product complaints, and inventory level fluctuations can be reported for months without being "flagged." This means that the individual executive can see information *if desired,* but it can remain in the background as long as it is within acceptable limits. When those limits are exceeded, the EIS automatically flags the item for immediate attention.

Leadership

Each executive appropriately discussed his or her leadership needs: more attention to quality, customer service, a greater sense of competitive urgency, and the need to constantly upgrade skills. Several executives described the importance of each salesperson in identifying shifts in the marketplace. Does the EIS have a role in enhancing our ability to lead the organization in these important directions?

The previous three categories of information address management's need to better understand and control the business and its resources. But information delivered electronically to executive management focuses the attention of its employees to a degree not attainable by paper reporting. This focused attention can be used to enhance the leadership message. If I know that customer service is receiving the highest level visibility, for example, I will quite naturally become more oriented toward customer service.

The Interview Results

The following details the interview results, which generally fall into seven categories:

Sales

Financial performance

Market research

Growth

Manufacturing

R & D

Human resources

This listing may suggest one possible organization for the EIS. The organization appropriate to MichTek may significantly differ from it.

Areas of particular concern are detailed in the following expanded list:

- *Sales performance*—as measured against all standards: product, account, region. Timeliness also needs to be improved. Reporting formats need to support early identification of unusual events and trends.

- *Account responsibility*—including important information on key accounts and bid data. This should also include customer compliance with contracts and affiliation with groups.

- *Service problems*—early and visible identification. An accompanying explanation of the problem is desirable, but should probably not be allowed to delay timely notification.

- *Account problems*—follows the same logic as service problems.

- *Financial performance*—the Brown book should be included. The Brown book should not be "delivered" at one time, but rather on a page-by-page basis, as available. Naturally, this category should also include performance against budget (including expenses).

- *Market research*—MichTek has amassed an impressive arsenal of material in this area. Delivery through the EIS could greatly enhance the usability of this information. Of special importance is the ability to rapidly explore potential issues using the market research data.

  Competitive intelligence is an important part of this category. Quick response to competitive action is critical. The quickest response is achieved by *anticipating* our competitor's next move. This requires not just open communication with the sales force (which MichTek already enjoys), but also a way to categorize and piece together otherwise unrelated bits of information.

- *Growth*—This deals with the strategic survival of MichTek. Unfortunately, the short term too often crowds out the seemingly "postponable" long term. Every executive shares the responsibility to constantly seek out new product and market opportunities. Because these opportunities may first show themselves as customer input, this category should be tied to both market research and sales.

  MichTek also needs to track progress toward product mix strategies and technical thrusts (such as new product development. Unfortunately, some of these strategic "directions" have no specific targets. For an organization as excellent as MichTek is, this should be viewed as unacceptable. If an objective is worthy (and this one is), it must be measured and tracked. The EIS is an excellent vehicle for such a purpose.

- *Human resources*—have been and will continue to be of critical importance to MichTek. Executive management needs to constantly provide leadership as to the importance of skill upgrades and hiring guidelines. The organization's responsiveness to these signals is typically a function of their visibility to management. As with technical thrusts, MichTek should establish and track progress toward training and recruiting requirements.

Recommended Priorities

There are several considerations in prioritizing EIS development. The ease of access and delivery of information must be weighed against (but not be allowed to dominate) the potential added value of critical categories. There is no single right answer. The recommendations included here should be considered a starting point, nothing more.

1. If the short term is not satisfied, there may never be a long term. For this reason, and the relative availability of the sales and (some) market research data, sales and market research information should be given the highest priority for delivery.

    By the same logic, the financial information can be given a high priority. Through the judicious use of information providers, MichTek should be able to make significant strides against these categories of information.

2. Service-level performance seemed to be of critical importance to all executives. This information seems to be available at a gross level, but this can hide many sins. Also, much of the information now provided is quite historical. It does little to provide early warning of emerging problems.

    Although the service level of older lines seems useful, there appears far too little emphasis on newer lines. This finding is not surprising, as newer lines represent a relatively small portion of the business. Since this has been targeted as a high-growth area, critical to the future of MichTek, it should probably receive more, not less attention.

3. Like service-level performance, most executives agreed that MichTek's future depends on the skill level of its employees, specifically those in sales. Yet management gets little (if any) regular information on progress toward skill upgrades. This is a critical but long-term priority.

4. Account information, including geographic performance, is vital to effective sales performance. MichTek should immediately begin to construct and deliver this information as it becomes available.

    The only reason this category is ranked fourth is that it might require significant resources (financial and personnel). This should not detract from its inclusion as a high-priority item. Account information should be given the highest development priority, but reality dictates that it will receive a secondary delivery priority, given the work involved.

All other items are not of a low priority. They can and should be delivered as they become available. The priorities suggested here are based upon the belief that survival dictates development order. That is, both tactical and strategic issues must be given highest priority. All other items will come on-line as soon as possible.

Detailed information is given below.

I. Robert Gray
   A. Existing Priority
      1. Monthly sales Results
      2. Field sales activity report
      3. Market research
         i. Demographics
         ii. Vertical markets
         iii. Retail
      4. Daily sheet (single sales number)
   B. Enhancements to Existing Information
      1. Ability to match market research information with sales resource deployment and performance.
      2. Assistance in selecting those products best presented to specific customers.
         i. This may not be an EIS application, but could be a high value expert system.
            a. Salesperson selects those characteristics most representative of the customer.
            b. The system is preset to filter in the specific products MichTek has interest in promoting.
            c. The salesperson then can select any other specific criteria.
            d. The system could be used prior to a sales call, or during the call itself.
      3. A "flash" report (perhaps every two weeks). This would bridge the gap between the daily sheet and monthly sales results.
      4. Geographic performance analysis.
      5. A published schedule of market research reports.
      6. Commentary added to market research.
         i. Market research tells what has happened, without much input as to *why* and *where*.

    C. Unmet Operational Requirements
1. Service-level performance
2. Service-level performance vs. competition
3. Mix of old line vs. new line
4. Price variations vs. competition

    D. Unmet Strategic Requirements
1. Customer service vs. competition
2. Quality of product
    i. This affects everyone. It is not just a manufacturing issue.
3. Monitoring how all departments affect the customer
4. Competitive intelligence
    i. Now this is received on a situation-by-situation basis. It is very difficult to develop patterns.
5. Performance against planned growth areas

II. Hank Travis

    A. Existing Priority
1. Sales by region/district
2. Customer quarterly sales
    i. 20% of customers produce 50% of business.
3. Expense management report
4. Daily sales report
5. Key correspondence

    B. Enhancements to Existing Information
1. Distributor sales
2. Regional sales
3. District sales
4. Customer sales

    C. Unmet Operational Requirements
1. Trade relations
2. Inventory at retail
3. Product availability
4. Status of forward buying
5. Frequency and number of calls
    i. This includes estimates of customer performance.
6. Shape of shelf space
    i. This could come from sales force.

    D. Unmet Strategic Requirements
1. Training of sales force to deal with multitude of product categories
2. Progress in educating consumer toward new line

III. Susan Grant

A. Existing Priority
  1. Daily sales
  2. Monthly sales and market share
  3. Customer attitude survey
  4. Competitive information
    i. Activity
    ii. Spending
    iii. Distribution channels
B. Enhancements to Existing Information
  1. Early identification of trends
    i. Ability to scan and filter large volumes of information.
C. Unmet Operational Requirements
  1. Training
    i. Sales training
    ii. RPC classes (assessment)
  2. Product improvements
  3. Customer complaints
D. Unmet Strategic Requirements
  1. Tracking progress toward move toward new lines

IV. Richard Dawkins
  A. Existing Priority
    1. Daily sales
    2. Calendar
    3. E-mail and other communications
    4. Personnel management
    5. Expense management report
    6. Sales ranking
    7. Customer attitude survey
    8. Market share
    9. Capital spending report
  B. Enhancements to Existing Information
    1. Pricing
  C. Unmet Operational Requirements
    1. New products
  D. Unmet Strategic Requirements
    1. Customer service
    2. Government intervention
    3. Market shifts

V. Stephen Walters
  A. Existing Priority
    1. Daily sales
    2. Budgets

    i. Exception
3. Field sales roster
4. Personnel
    i. Number of people
    ii. Sales force personnel report
    iii. Field turnover
5. Accidents
B. Enhancements to Existing Information
    1. Faster information on promotional spending
    2. Quick highlighting of accounts in trouble
        i. Early warning system
    3. Directory of voice-com addresses
    4. Field sales roster on-line
C. Unmet Operational Requirements
    1. Lead indicators of change in sales force requirements
    2. Training
        i. Sales training
    3. Product improvements
    4. Customer complaints
    5. Early warning of out-of-stock conditions
D. Unmet Strategic Requirements
    1. New product success
    2. Loyalty from new customers
VI. Marv Raston
A. Existing Priority
    1. Customer attitude survey
    2. Pay package information
    3. Personnel
        i. Accidents
        ii. Performance problems
        iii. Direct expense usage
    4. Performance monitoring
B. Enhancements to Existing Information
    1. Territory-level reporting
    2. Impact of sales presentations on customer
    3. Better personnel information
C. Unmet Operational Requirements
D. Unmet Strategic Requirements
    1. Consumer marketing
VIII. Suggestions
A. Competition

      1. Provide access to items in the "Competitive Activity News-
letter," allowing viewing by competitor, category (advertising, sales, pricing, service) and region.

    B. Customer Satisfaction

      1. Overall service is currently measured. Other items, how-
ever, are not consistently measured and tracked.

      These items do not all require interviews and surveys.
Much of this information can be tracked internally. This
allows for an improved proactive stance.

Details by Category

I. Categories

  A. Sales

    1. Trade relations
    2. Monthly sales
    3. Daily Sales
    4. Field sales activity report
    5. Match mkt. resch. w/ sales
    6. Match products w/ customers
    7. Bimonthly sales
    8. Geographic perform. analysis
    9. Field office expenses
   10. Shape of shelf space
   11. Inventory at retail
   12. Frequency and number of calls
   13. Customer quarterly sales
   14. European sales expense
   15. Market share
   16. European sales
   17. Regional sales
   18. Expense as % sales
   19. Top 25 accounts by business

  B. Market Research

    1. Trade relations
    2. Match mkt. resch. w/sales
    3. Add commentary to mkt. resch.
    4. Published sched. of MR reports
    5. Customer attitude survey
    6. Market share

  C. Competitive Intelligence

    1. Svc.-level perform. vs. compet
    2. Price variations vs. compet.
    3. Access to comp. activ. news
D. Service-level performance
    1. Trade relations
    2. Svc.-level perform. vs. compet.
    3. Quality of product
    4. Out-of-stock conditions
E. Early Warning
    1. Svc.-level perform. vs. compet.
    2. Price variations vs. compet.
    3. Quality of product
    4. Out-of-stock conditions
    5. Shape of shelf space
    6. Inventory at retail
    7. Frequency and number of calls
    8. Returns by return code
F. Performance to budget
    1. Monthly sales
    2. Geographic perform. analysis
    3. Mix of new lines vs. old lines
    4. Customer quarterly sales
    5. Expense trackg.
    6. Expense as % sales
    7. More current expense reporting
G. Personnel
    1. Sales force training
    2. Personnel report
    3. Merit planning
    4. Supervisory visit repts.
    5. Sales force roster
    6. More current pers. rept.
    7. Fleet car exceptions
    8. Voice-com directory
    9. Field office expenses as % sales
    10. Top 25 accounts by business
    11. Promotion expense trackg.
    12. Sales training expense
H. Performance to Long Range Plan
    1. Trade relations
    2. Market research data

3. Geographic perform. analysis
4. Mix of new products vs. old products
5. Quality of product
6. Sales force training
7. Access to comp. activ. news

I. Key Correspondence

Appendix B   Selection of EIS Articles

How to Use the References

This appendix lists articles on EIS, most published over the past few years. These articles were selected because of their references to organizations and applications, covering a wide variety of industries, both private and public. In the first section, for each article you will find a list indicating the referenced organizations and whether the article covers EIS benefits or executive testimony.

I suggest that you use the first section, "Reference Articles," to find those articles most appropriate to your goal of introducing executives to the EIS concept. To assist you in this, you will find subsequent sections in which the articles are listed according to those addressing benefits and executive testimony (direct quotes on how other executives use EIS).

Finally, I have also included an alphabetized listing of organizations, with lists of the articles in which they are mentioned. I hope this material will be helpful as you prepare your executive presentations, in addition to providing you some introductory material to use prior to the interview.

REFERENCE ARTICLES

1. "At Last, Software CEOs Can Use," Jeremy Main, *Fortune,* March 13, 1989, referring to

- Duracell
- Executive testimony
- Benefits
- Northwest Airlines
- Westinghouse
- Citizens & Southern
- General Electric
- Grumman
- Kraft
- John Hancock
- Metropolitan Life
- Bank of Boston
- Boeing
- Marine Midland
- Monsanto
- Public Service Electric & Gas
- Unum Life
- ConAgra
- Johnson & Johnson
- Phillips Petroleum
- Xerox
- Dupont
- GTE

2. "Prototype That EIS," Larry Runge, *Information Center,* February 1989, referring to:
   - GE Aerospace
3. "The Executive Use of Workstations," Richard L. Crandall, *Information Strategy,* Spring, 1986, referring to:
   - Benefits
4. "Point of Access," Leila Davis, *Datamation,* July 15, 1989, referring to:
   - Teleglobe Canada, Inc.
   - Central and Southwest
5. "Frito-Lay Rewrites EIS History Using Regional LANs," Dennis Eskow, *Management,* February 26, 1990, referring to:
   - Frito-Lay
6. "Attractive Graphics Can Lead to Good Publicity," Len Strazewski, *City & State,* December 4, 1989, referring to:
   - State of Washington
7. "Executive Information Systems Help Senior Management to Manage the Bank," *Bank Operations Report,* November, 1989, referring to:
   - North Carolina National Bank
   - Benefits

8. "Helping Executives Get the Computer Data They Need," Laton McCartney, *Dun's Business Month,* May, 1989, referring to:
   - Gould, Inc.
   - Benefits
   - Executive testimony
9. "High-Impact EIS," Kathleen Melymuka, *CIO,* February, 1989, referring to:
   - The New England
   - Benefits
   - Executive testimony
   - Xerox
10. "Information Powers", *InformationWeek,* October 9, 1989, referring to:
    - Computer industry
    - Du Pont
    - Executive testimony
    - GE Capital
    - Hertz
11. "EIS Lets Telcos Monitor Service at a Glance," Roseanne Shanks, *Telephone Engineer & Management,* October 15, 1989, referring to:
    - Cincinnati Bell Telephone
    - Executive testimony
12. "Going Beyond Number Crunching," Laton McCartney, *Corporate Finance,* March, 1989, referring to:
    - Kraft
    - McNeil Pharmaceutical
13. "Special Systems Make Computing Less Traumatic for Top Executives," William Bulkeley, *The Wall Street Journal,* June 20, 1988, referring to:
    - Benefits
    - Executive testimony
    - Bank of Boston
    - Avon Products
    - American Telephone & Telegraph
    - Polaroid Corporation
14. "Putting Hertz Executives in the Driver's Seat," Meghan O'Leary, *CIO,* February, 1990, referring to:
    - Hertz
    - Executive testimony
    - Benefits
15. "EIS in the Federal Government: Designing to Win," Kristin Knauth, *Government Executive,* February, 1990, referring to:
    - Defense Department

- Benefits
- Commerce Department
- GSA
16. "One Step Ahead," Gerry Blackwell, *Office Automation,* February, 1990, referring to:
- Du Pont Canada
- Benefits
17. "Executives Go High Tech," Michael Gauthier, *Business Month,* July, 1989, referring to:
- Benefits
- Hertz
- Bank of Boston
18. "The Computer Age Dawns in the Corner Office," Susan Gelfond, *BusinessWeek,* June 27, 1988, referring to:
- Kraft
- Benefits
- Executive testimony
- Phillips Petroleum
- The New England
- Coca-Cola
19. "Info Made Easy for Top Execs," Catherine Lynch, *ComputerData,* September, 1989, referring to:
- Teleglobe Canada, Inc.
- Benefits

BENEFITS

1. "At Last, Software CEOs Can Use," Jeremy Main, *Fortune,* March 13, 1989.

2. "The Executive Use of Workstations," Richard L. Crandall, *Information Strategy,* Spring, 1986.

3. "Putting Hertz Executives in the Driver's Seat," Meghan O'Leary, *CIO,* February, 1990.

4. "EIS in the Federal Government: Designing to Win," Kristin Knauth, *Government Executive,* February, 1990.

5. "One Step Ahead," Gerry Blackwell, *Office Automation,* February, 1990.

6. "Computers Move from Backroom to Boardroom," *The Economist,* July 23, 1988.

7. "Executives Go High Tech," Michael Gauthier, *Business Month,* July, 1989.

8. "The Computer Age Dawns in the Corner Office," Susan Gelfond, *BusinessWeek,* June 27, 1988.

9. "Info Made Easy for Top Execs," Catherine Lynch, *ComputerData,* September, 1989.

10. "Executive Information Systems Help Senior Management to Manage the Bank," *Bank Operations Report,* November, 1989.

11. "Helping Executives Get the Computer Data They Need," Laton McCartney, *Dun's Business Month,* May, 1989.

12. "High-Impact EIS," Kathleen Melymuka, *CIO*, February, 1989.

13. "Special Systems Make Computing Less Traumatic for Top Executives," William Bulkeley, *The Wall Street Journal,* June 20, 1988.

EXECUTIVE TESTIMONY

1. "At Last, Software CEOs Can Use," Jeremy Main, *Fortune,* March 13, 1989.

2. "Information Powers," *InformationWeek,* October 9, 1989.

3. "EIS Lets Telcos Monitor Service at a Glance," Roseanne Shanks, *Telephone Engineer & Management,* October 15, 1989.

4. "Putting Hertz Executives in the Driver's Seat," Meghan O'Leary, *CIO,* February, 1990.

5. "The Computer Age Dawns in the Corner Office," Susan Gelfond, *BusinessWeek,* June 27, 1988.

6. "Helping Executives Get the Computer Data They Need," Laton McCartney, *Dun's Business Month,* May, 1989.

7. "High-Impact EIS," Kathleen Melymuka, *CIO,* February, 1989.

8. "Special Systems Make Computing Less Traumatic for Top Executives," William Bulkeley, *The Wall Street Journal,* June 20, 1988.

ORGANIZATIONS

ADT
- "Computers Move From Backroom to Boardroom," *The Economist,* July 23, 1988.

American Cyanamid Company
- "ExecTech," *Business Software Review,* July, 1987.

American Telephone & Telegraph
- "Special Systems Make Computing Less Traumatic for Top Executives," William Bulkeley, *The Wall Street Journal,* June 20, 1988.

Avon
- "Special Systems Make Computing Less Traumatic for Top Executives," William Bulkeley, *The Wall Street Journal,* June 20, 1988.

Bank of Boston
- "At Last, Software CEOs Can Use," Jeremy Main, *Fortune,* March 13, 1989.

- "Executives Go High Tech," Michael Gauthier, *Business Month,* July, 1989.

- "Special Systems Make Computing Less Traumatic for Top Executives," William Bulkeley, *The Wall Street Journal,* June 20, 1988.

Boeing
- "At Last, Software CEOs Can Use," Jeremy Main, *Fortune,* March 13, 1989.

Central and Southwest
- "Point of Access," Leila Davis, *Datamation,* July 15, 1989.

Cincinnati Bell Telephone
- "EIS Lets Telcos Monitor Service at a Glance," Roseanne Shanks, *Telephone Engineer & Management,* October 15, 1989.

Citizens & Southern
- "At Last, Software CEOs Can Use," Jeremy Main, *Fortune,* March 13, 1989.

Coca-Cola
- "The Computer Age Dawns in the Corner Office," Susan Gelfond, *BusinessWeek,* June 27, 1988.

Commerce Department
- "EIS in the Federal Government: Designing to Win," Kristin Knauth, *Government Executive,* February, 1990.

ConAgra
- "At Last, Software CEOs Can Use," Jeremy Main, *Fortune,* March 13, 1989.

Defense Department
- "EIS in the Federal Government: Designing to Win," Kristin Knauth, *Government Executive,* February, 1990.

Du Pont
- "Information Powers," *InformationWeek,* October 9, 1989.
- "At Last, Software CEOs Can Use," Jeremy Main, *Fortune,* March 13, 1989.

Du Pont Canada
- "One Step Ahead," Gerry Blackwell, *Office Automation,* February, 1990.

Duracell
- "At Last, Software CEOs Can Use," Jeremy Main, *Fortune,* March 13, 1989.

Frito-Lay
- "Frito-Lay Rewrites EIS History Using Regional LANs," Dennis Eskow, *Management,* February 26, 1990.

GE Aerospace
- "Prototype That EIS," Larry Runge, *Information Center,* February 1989.

GE Capital
- "Information Powers", *InformationWeek,* October 9, 1989.

General Electric
- "At Last, Software CEOs Can Use," Jeremy Main, *Fortune,* March 13, 1989.

Gould, Inc.
- "Helping Executives Get the Computer Data They Need," Laton McCartney, *Dun's Business Month,* May, 1989.

Grumman
- "At Last, Software CEOs Can Use," Jeremy Main, *Fortune,* March 13, 1989.

GSA
- "EIS in the Federal Government: Designing to Win," Kristin Knauth, *Government Executive,* February, 1990.

GTE
- "At Last, Software CEOs Can Use," Jeremy Main, *Fortune,* March 13, 1989.

Hertz
- "Information Powers," *InformationWeek,* October 9, 1989.

- "Putting Hertz Executives in the Driver's Seat," Meghan O'Leary, *CIO,* February, 1990.

- "Executives Go High Tech," Michael Gauthier, *Business Month*, July, 1989.

John Hancock
- "At Last, Software CEOs Can Use," Jeremy Main, *Fortune,* March 13, 1989.

Johnson & Johnson
- "At Last, Software CEOs Can Use," Jeremy Main, *Fortune,* March 13, 1989.

Kraft
- "At Last, Software CEOs Can Use," Jeremy Main, *Fortune,* March 13, 1989.

- "Going Beyond Number Crunching," Laton McCartney, *Corporate Finance,* March, 1989.

- "The Computer Age Dawns in the Corner Office," Susan Gelfond, *BusinessWeek,* June 27, 1988.

Marine Midland
- "At Last, Software CEOs Can Use," Jeremy Main, *Fortune,* March 13, 1989.

McNeil Pharmaceutical
- "Going Beyond Number Crunching," Laton McCartney, *Corporate Finance,* March, 1989.

Metropolitan Life
- "At Last, Software CEOs Can Use," Jeremy Main, *Fortune,* March 13, 1989.

Monsanto
- "At Last, Software CEOs Can Use," Jeremy Main, *Fortune,* March 13, 1989.

Mrs. Fields Cookies
- "Computers Move from Backroom to Boardroom," *The Economist,* July 23, 1988.

New England Mutual Life
- "Computers Move from Backroom to Boardroom," *The Economist,* July 23, 1988.

North Carolina National Bank
- "Executive Information Systems Help Senior Management to Manage the Bank," *Bank Operations Report,* November, 1989.

Northwest Airlines
- "At Last, Software CEOs Can Use," Jeremy Main, *Fortune,* March 13, 1989

Phillips Petroleum
- "At Last, Software CEOs Can Use," Jeremy Main, *Fortune,* March 13, 1989.

- "The Computer Age Dawns in the Corner Office," Susan Gelfond, *BusinessWeek,* June 27, 1988.

Polaroid Corporation
- "Special Systems Make Computing Less Traumatic for Top Executives," William Bulkeley, *The Wall Street Journal,* June 20, 1988.

Public Service Electric & Gas
- "At Last, Software CEOs Can Use," Jeremy Main, *Fortune,* March 13, 1989.

State of Washington
- "Attractive Graphics Can Lead to Good Publicity," Len Strazewski, *City & State,* December 4, 1989.

Teleglobe Canada, Inc.
- "Info Made Easy for Top Execs," Catherine Lynch, *ComputerData,* September, 1989.

- "Point of Access," Leila Davis, *Datamation,* July 15, 1989.

The New England
- "The Computer Age Dawns in the Corner Office," Susan Gelfond, *BusinessWeek,* June 27, 1988.

- "High-Impact EIS," Kathleen Melymuka, *CIO,* February, 1989.

Unum Corporation
- "Special Systems Make Computing Less Traumatic for Top Executives," William Bulkeley, *The Wall Street Journal,* June 20, 1988.

Unum Life
- "At Last, Software CEOs Can Use," Jeremy Main, *Fortune,* March 13, 1989.

Westinghouse
- "At Last, Software CEOs Can Use," Jeremy Main, *Fortune,* March 13, 1989.

Xerox
- "At Last, Software CEOs Can Use," Jeremy Main, *Fortune,* March 13, 1989.

- "High-Impact EIS," Kathleen Melymuka, *CIO,* February, 1989.

- "Special Systems Make Computing Less Traumatic for Top Executives," William Bulkeley, *The Wall Street Journal,* June 20, 1988.

Index